# HOW TO HAUNT A HOUSE FOR HALLOWEEN

# HOW TO HAUNT A HOUSE FOR HALLOWEEN

BY FRIEDHOFFER
THE MADMAN OF MAGIC
with Harriet Brown

Illustrated by Richard Kaufman
Photographs by Timothy White

Franklin Watts
New York/London/Toronto/Sydney/1988

Library of Congress Cataloging-in-Publication Data

Friedhoffer, Robert.
How to haunt a house for Halloween/by Friedhoffer, the madman of magic, with Harriet Brown; illustrated by Richard Kaufman; photographs by Timothy White.
p. cm.
Bibliography: p.
Includes index.
Summary: Provides tips on how to create a haunted house at home and instructions for performing magic tricks at a Halloween party.
ISBN 0-531-15122-0 (paper ed.) — ISBN 0-531-10501-6 (lib. bdg.)
1. Halloween decorations—Juvenile literature. [1. Halloween decorations. 2. Parties. 3. Magic tricks.] I. Brown, Harriet.
II. Kaufman, Richard, ill. III. Title.
TT900.H32F75 1988
790.1'922—dc19 87-27990 CIP AC


Printed in the United States of America
6

# CONTENTS

TO NIKKI RAE FRIEDHOFFER—
THE REAL MAGIC IN MY LIFE

Thanks to the following folks
for their help and encouragement:
Cisco Ward; Abbi Lindner; Tim White;
Richard Kaufman; Tommy Ladshaw; Mark Phillips;
Harvey Klinger; Neal Hollander;
Jeff, Carol, Beth, Adam, and Randy Friedhoffer;
Steve Rodman, Joe Silkie;
Brian, Matt, and the gang at BWI;
Iris Rosoff; Robert Baxt;
Jennie Parrish, Phillip Namanworth.

# A NOTE FROM THE AUTHORS

We've included tricks that we felt were appropriate for children.

We've tried to gear these effects so that they are, above all, not dangerous.

We have included a few that are difficult, but still within the abilities of a determined and creative child.

WHO: Anyone between the ages of eight and eighty-eight.

WHAT: A room or series of rooms designed to scare, frighten, bewilder, and bedevil your friends.

WHY: To quicken the heartbeat and cause the sweat to flow, to frighten your friends in time-honored ways, and to have fun!

WHERE: Your house, a storefront, a basement, an alleyway, a backyard—use your imagination! You can haunt just about any place.

WHEN: Fall is the time for witches, goblins, skeletons, and the like, when the leaves are changing, apples are ripening, and Halloween is just around the corner.

# SO YOU WANT TO HAUNT A HOUSE

There are many good reasons why you might want to haunt a house. People *love* to feel frightened and are even willing to pay for the privilege. That's why so many people go to horror movies and ride the really scary rides at amusement parks. And that's why they love haunted houses.

A haunted house is also a great way to raise money for a good cause. It's fun for the haunters as well as the hauntees—it's always a thrill to watch people's faces when they're getting the scare of their lives. Whether you want to haunt your living room or a school auditorium, this book will tell you everything you need to know and a few more things besides. We'll give you a checklist for organized haunting, tell you how and where to collect your materials, give you some good tips on telling ghost stories, and tell you how to perform some of the scariest tricks we know. Just remember—the most important thing is to have fun!

# GETTING READY

Haunting a house takes a lot of planning. You will have to make many decisions. First you must decide where and when the haunting will take place. Then you need to figure out what kind of haunted house you want. We're going to give you lots of ideas; some of them will make your hair stand on end. It might be a good idea to read this book with a pencil and paper handy, jotting down the things that you like best.

One very important item on the list of preparations is checking with the person in charge of your haunted house, whether it's your parents, the school principal, or the pastor of your church. Let the person know just what you're planning to do and what it will involve. You don't want to get halfway through your project and have your parents stop you because what you're doing is too scary, too messy, or too expensive. *None of these tricks or illusions is dangerous.* Nevertheless, you should get permission before you begin.

One way to plan your haunted house with the least possible mayhem (except when you want it, of course!) is to draw a floor plan of the rooms you're going to use. This is a good way to make sure everything will fit into the rooms before you go to the trouble of building or preparing something. It's not complicated tricks that make a great haunted house, but how *well* the tricks work. It's better to try something a little less ambitious that *works* than to try to produce a complicated effect and fail. One way to make sure your effects are going to work is to practice them, preferably on a willing audience.

Let's say you've read through this book and jotted down a list of the tricks you want to use in your haunted house. You've checked them out with your parents and drawn up your floor plan, and you now have a

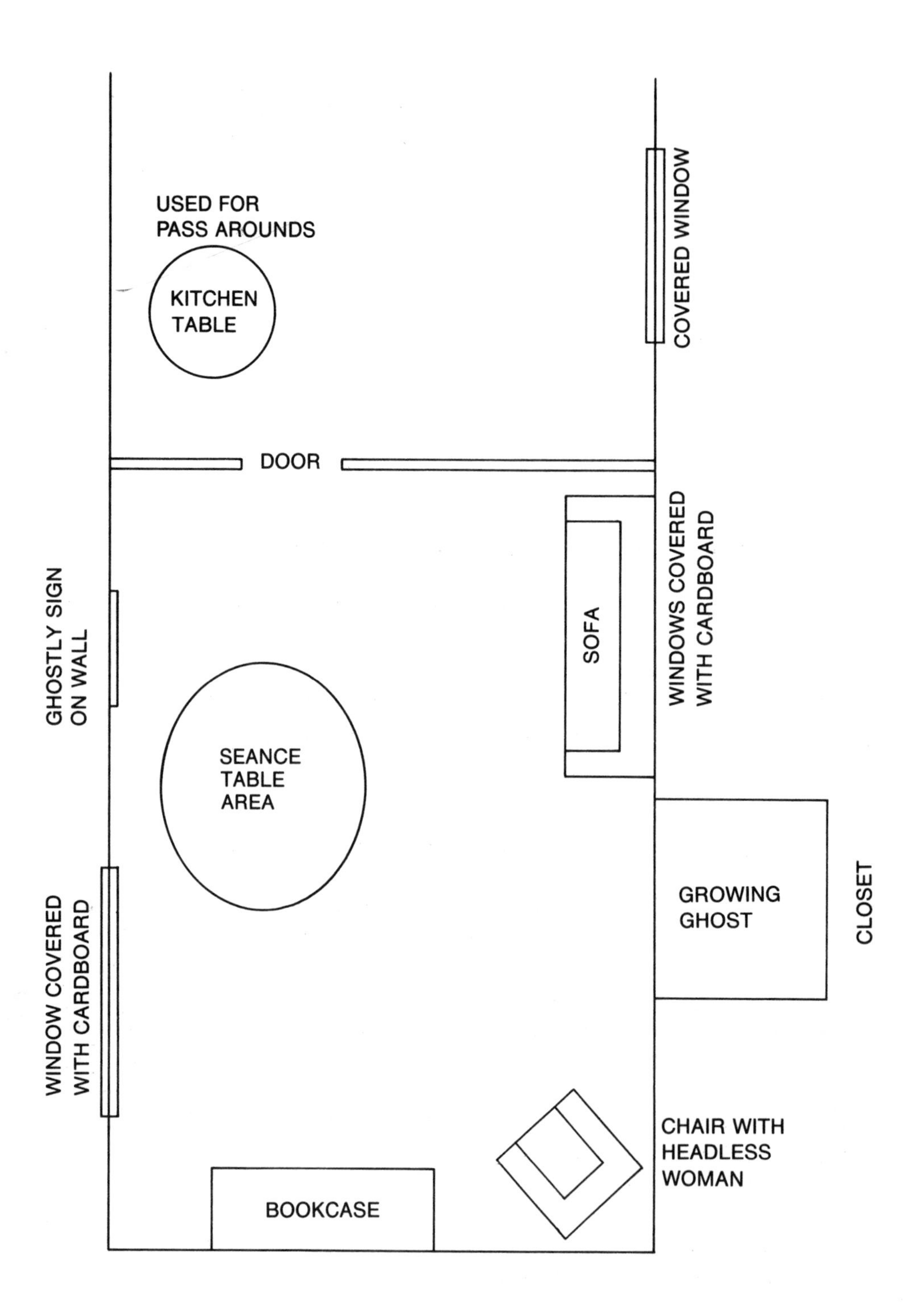
USED FOR
PASS AROUNDS
KITCHEN
TABLE
COVERED WINDOW
DOOR
WINDOWS COVERED
WITH CARDBOARD
SOFA
GHOSTLY SIGN
ON WALL
SEANCE
TABLE
AREA
GROWING
GHOST
CLOSET
WINDOW COVERED
WITH CARDBOARD
CHAIR WITH
HEADLESS
WOMAN
BOOKCASE

FLOOR PLAN

general idea of where everything will go. The next thing to do is plan your guest list. You can use a format something like this:

| NAME | INVITATION GIVEN | ACCEPTED? |
|---|---|---|
| Joe Collins | October 14 | Yes |
| Dawn Redding | October 14 | Yes |
| Lisa Ann Bornstein | October 15 | Yes (bringing cupcakes) |
| Pamela Reilly | October 15 | No (someone else to bring soda?) |
| Jack Dobson | October 16 | Yes (bringing vampire mask) |

Once you have invited your guests, you can decide what kind of refreshments to serve and how to arrange your special effects to their best advantage.

## MAKING THE ROOM DARK

Most of the effects we will describe in this book depend on darkness. A dark room will make your guests think about witches, goblins, and things that go bump in the night. In other words, it will make your friends more receptive to the surprises you have in store for them. So it's important that you know how to make a room truly dark. There are tricks that depend on the room being *pitch black;* we've indicated those. If you were doing this professionally, we'd recommend that the windows be painted black. However, this might be tough to explain to Mom and Dad. The next best way to darken the room is to place blackout material over all the windows. You can make blackout material from pieces of corrugated cardboard cartons cut to fit tightly over all windows and held in place with masking tape, cellophane tape, or thumbtacks. When you set up your blackout materials, be very careful that you don't arrange them in such a way that you will end up peeling the paint from the walls when you take them down. You can also cover windows and doors with towels, blankets, or any other heavy material. Remember to try it first and make sure that whatever you're using really blocks out most or all of the light.

DARKENING THE ROOM

## SETTING THE MOOD

Before you try your most spectacular haunting, it's important to put your victims in the right mood. Start the party off right by playing spooky music or the music from a suspense film that everyone is familiar with like *Close Encounters of the Third Kind.* Around Halloween time there are special records and tapes available just to set the mood. Check record stores and even five-and-tens. Have the lights turned down low and your special blackout effects in place.

Serve refreshments to your guests, carefully labeled so that even the most strong-stomached friends are revolted. For example, a punch bowl of grape juice can be called Bat Blood. Olives can be Frogs' Bodies. Potato chips are Zombie Ears. Hamburgers are Ghoul Sandwiches, smothered in fresh Zombie Blood (ketchup). Hot dogs will be Witches' Fingers, covered with Witch Bile (mustard) and Ghoul Hair (sauerkraut). Popcorn is Ground Baby Bats. You get the idea.

Read your victims some stories to put them in the mood; some of the most frightening horror stories are still some of the old classics, like the best of H. P. Lovecraft, Edgar Allan Poe, and H. G. Wells. (See For Further Reading, a more complete list.)

## PREPARING THE SCRIPT

Your victims—we mean audience—are now ready for the show to begin. Have everyone sit in a circle, with the lights and music down low. You are now ready to begin. You will start with a script. Of course, you won't really be reading from a piece of paper. What we mean by a script is a ghost story or a few stories that you have practiced telling until you can tell them in the most frightening and authentic way. We all know that actors rehearse their lines, and *you* are doing quite an acting job!

To tell a scary story well, you will have to rehearse it, just as you practice an instrument or a sport. There are a couple of things you have to remember before you begin, and after that, it's just a question of refining your technique. There are five basic elements in telling a good ghost story:

- Atmosphere
- Quality
- Personal details
- Familiar places
- Drama

Creating the right *atmosphere* is very, very important. We can't stress this enough! In a dark room, people will be very sensitive to anything you suggest. No, you can't make them bark like dogs, but you can make them believe that the simple things they hear and touch are really frightful messages from another world. The least little thing will frighten your audience. You can establish the atmosphere for them by preparing the room. Turn the lights down low, play spooky music in the background, think up ghoulish names for the refreshments, and use a scary tone of voice when you speak. Your victims will almost literally scare themselves! If you're doing this in the fall, you can start things off right by reminding them that Halloween is the night when ghosts, goblins, witches, and zombies come out of their caves and graves to cause mischief.

Even a well-told story can flop if the atmosphere isn't spooky or if the story itself just isn't frightening enough. This may sound obvious, but it's as important to keep in mind when you're organizing your haunted house as is the physical preparation of the rooms.

*Quality* means keeping your story on as high a level as possible. Don't use trite material; maintain a high standard in choosing and telling your story.

Once you've picked out a good story, you should add to it as many *personal details* as possible. You do this by telling the tale as if it happened to someone you all know or someone related to you. For example, you might begin a story by saying, "This happened twenty years ago when our neighbors, the Fishers, had just moved into their house. It seems that one night Mrs. Fisher . . ." If your audience identifies with the people in the story, it will make it all the more real to them.

You should also mention *familiar places* in your story. Make it occur as close to home as possible. You can even have the action take place in the very room you're sitting in. This will raise the hairs on the back of everyone's neck. If the building you're in is new, tell the story as if it happened in an old building that once stood on the same site. You could say, for example, that an old, unsolved murder was committed on this very property. This is where your imagination comes in!

Last, but not least, you must add *drama* to the story by mentioning many gory, horrifying details. Another way to dramatize a story effectively is to use sound effects. (We'll talk more about sound effects later.) You can record some frightening sounds on a tape recorder and have someone play them back while you're telling the story. You can also have an assistant hiding in the wings, making the noises as you tell the story. The tone of your voice has a great effect on your audience, too; by lowering your voice to a whisper and then suddenly screaming, you put your audience into the proper frame of mind and maybe even turn a few hairs white.

Here is a sample ghost story with hints on how to tell it effectively:

> *Twenty years ago, in this very house, a death took place, and this house has been haunted ever since.* (You look around the room). *A young boy—oh, just about our age—was playing with his friends one rainy night right in this very room. They were sitting on the floor over there* (point). *The boys and girls heard a knock at the door.* (Your assistant knocks on the wall.) *Their parents had warned them never to answer the door or open it to strangers. But* (your voice sinks to a whisper) *they didn't listen. And they didn't know that a convict had escaped from the jail on that very night and was looking for a hideout.*
>
> *The children opened the door* (your assistant opens it slowly from the other side), *and the convict came in. He was starving and exhausted from running from the police, and in the confusion, the kids managed to escape. They ran out the door, down the hall* (sound of thudding footsteps from the hallway) *and out into the darkness, and they kept running until they reached the next house. They burst into the kitchen and told the neighbors what had happened, but the grown-ups didn't believe them. They did call the police, though, when they saw how upset the children were.*
>
> *The police, who knew about the convict escaping, rushed over to the house with their sirens wailing.* (Your assistant plays a tape of police sirens.) *The convict, realizing that the police were on their way to get him, ran to the kitchen, took a big knife from a drawer* (you brandish a rubber knife), *and barricaded himself in the room. The police broke through to the room where he was hiding, shivering and exhausted, and stood outside the door. Open up in there! We have the house surrounded!* (You shout suddenly.) *When the convict didn't reply, the police broke down the door.* (Assistant makes scuffling noises and then a loud crash.) *Desperate now, the convict held up the knife* (you do so) *and rushed at one of the policemen. But the intruder was so weak that he collapsed halfway across the room, fell, and* (your voice drops to a whisper) *impaled himself on his own knife, right through his heart.*

*Ever since that night, strange things have happened in this house from time to time. To this day, if you look carefully, you can see a large bloodstain on the floor where the convict died* (you point to where someone is seated on the floor). *The people who lived here moved away because their children suffered terrible nightmares every night. They would wake up screaming about a knife. My parents moved years later. And even they don't know this story.*

Often other people in your audience will have scary stories of their own to tell, and you could wind up being scared by a few yourself! If you're interested in another good horror story, try this one out on your willing listeners:

*Not too long ago, I went to visit some friends of my parents who had a big old farmhouse in the country. I was so excited about going that I took along my baseball glove, baseball hat, a bat, my new red striped bathing suit, a camera, and some other stuff. When I got there, Mr. and Mrs. Langan showed me around the house and barn. They had pigs, chickens—even a tractor, which I got to drive! After dinner, we watched TV together, and then I went up to sleep. At least, I tried to.*

*I had just started to drift off when I felt a cold breeze on my face. I got up to make sure the window was closed—and it was. But I still felt gusts of cold air blowing on my face. I pulled the covers up around my head, and just then I heard a voice, right beside the bed. It was whispering my name!*

*I didn't hear anything for a few seconds, so I stuck my head out and looked around. Nothing was there. I jumped out of bed and got my baseball bat out of the bag where I had thrown it in the corner. I wanted it in bed with me, in case someone was really in the room. Suddenly, I heard footsteps right by my bed. "Who's there?" I asked. No one answered; there was just another blast of cold wind coming from nowhere.*

*Then I saw the camera by my bed. I took three flash pictures of the room—I don't know why, but it made me feel better. When I finally fell asleep that night, the rooster was already crowing.*

*The next morning I told the Langans what I had heard. They gave each other the strangest look. Then Mrs. Langan told me that fifty years before, in that very room, a young woman had gone mad. They were convinced that I had heard her ghost. I switched rooms and had a great time for the rest of my visit.*

*A couple of weeks after I got home, I had the film in my camera developed. The first three pictures on the roll showed an ordinary room—the room I had first slept in on my visit. Ordinary, except that right in the middle of the room stood a ghostly woman, her hair wild, her eyes dazed. Note: The ghost in the photograph is not a bearded lady, but the author.*

If you want to make this story even scarier, you can whip out a carefully prepared photograph at this point, a double exposure of someone's mother or sister in a long white nightgown. The double exposure makes the picture look ghostly. (Make sure when you take the photograph that the camera is on a tripod and stays absolutely still.)

## PREPARING PASS-AROUNDS

Now that your victims are nice and frightened, it's a good time to do what we call pass-arounds. This will be a preliminary to the actual tricks and effects you will perform. The more preparation you give the audience in the way of these pass-arounds and stories, the more frightened they will be, and the more successful your illusions and tricks. If you are unable to make or build any of these items, check the list of suppliers in the back of this book for sources of novelties or gags. Remember, the best atmosphere for pass-arounds, or any other effect, is a darkened or dimly lit room.

Begin by passing around a skull—the kind you can buy at a novelty store or make from papier-mâché, or see the list of suppliers at the back of this book.

Next, pass around a zombie's finger bones. Save all the bones from chicken thighs. After your family has eaten the meat, scrape the bones clean, boil them in water, and let them dry. Tell this story while you're passing the bones around:

*The zombie's finger bones come from Russoslavia. When my uncle was in the merchant marines, he went all over the world. One afternoon he was in the town of Slovestsky enjoying a beer at a dockside tavern, when he heard a commotion in a nearby alleyway. He rushed out to find an old man being beat-*

GHOSTLY DOUBLE EXPOSURE

*en by thugs. Being a warm-hearted soul, my uncle went to the man's aid. Afterward, the grateful old-timer, who was really a warlock, gave my uncle these bones and told him that as long as he had them in his possession no harm would come to him. My uncle told me the story and left the bones with me. The next day he went to sea and his ship sank with no survivors.*

Next pass around a witch's scalp and hair. You can use an old wig, crepe hair that has been separated, steamed, and ironed flat, or even some strands from an old mop. Glue the ends of the "hair" to a thin sheet of leather or flexible plastic and you've got your scalp. While you're passing this around, you can tell the story of how a witch left behind this piece of her scalp as she was riding by your chimney on her broomstick. Say that a bat jumped out and frightened her, and her broomstick went out of control, bumping into the chimney. The witch smacked her head on a brick and left behind this piece of her hair and scalp as a souvenir.

Here's another story you can tell as you pass the hair around the room:

*One day my grandfather was walking in the field behind our house when a witch rode by. She decided to steal his soul as a present for the devil, because she had a terrible crush on him. My grandfather was a god-fearing man; when he saw the witch, he began to pray. The witch swooped down, laughing* (your assistant makes a devilish cackle), *but Grandpa stood his ground. He reached up and grabbed his soul back from between the witch's fingers. A lock of her hair got tangled up in his fingers, and he ripped it right out of her head!*

Next bring out a shoebox with holes punched in the top. "This is my pet rat, Igor," you announce in a mysterious voice. "He wasn't always a rat; he used to be my assistant. Igor was helping me with some very important lab experiments last week. Unfortunately, he drank the potion before I could stop him. If enough people pet him, Igor might just turn back into a human being." Let people reach into the box and touch Igor. Of course, you won't have a real rat in the box. A piece of rabbit fur or fake fur cut to about 4 by 8 inches will do nicely. Drop some glue on several spots on the fur and let it harden; your friends will swear they are feeling teeth and claws.

For a grand finale, pass around a bowl of blood. (We'll tell you how to make "blood" later on.) This stuff is *very* messy; once you get it on your clothes or on the rug or drapes, it might not come out, so *be careful.* Have your guests place their hands in the bowl without seeing what it is. When they pull them out, covered in "blood," they'll be terrified! Tell them this is the blood from a nearby slaughterhouse: "Normally they slaughter chickens, but I heard that yesterday one of the workmen slipped into the machine." Be sure to pass around a bowl of warm water and a roll of paper towels afterward, so your guests can clean their hands right away.

Now the stage is set for you to play your trump card: your stock of magic tricks and scary illusions.

## CHECKLIST

- □ Time and place
- □ Parent's approval
- □ List of tricks and effects
- □ Floor plan
- □ Guest list
- □ List of helpers
- □ Costumes
- □ Script, with sound effects prepared
- □ Pass-arounds

# TABLEAUX

When you draw up your floor plan, one of the things you may want to include is a room or series of rooms with scary tableaux, or scenes. As your audience walks through these rooms, it gets them into a pleasantly terrified state of mind!

Remember to have everything set up *before* people start to walk through the rooms. It would be best if you personally escorted your audience through the rooms. In this way, you can prevent them from touching anything and possibly ruining the tableau. Remember, it's *very* important to have these rooms dimly lit.

Here are some of our favorite frightening scenes. They're all easy to set up, and when presented well, they will really scare your friends! You will need your assistant for all of these.

## THE ELONGATING GHOST

*What You'll Need*

One plastic or aluminum bowl
One stick about 3 feet long (a yardstick will do)
One white sheet, about 10 feet long and 6 feet wide, sewn into a 10 foot tube, closed at one end and open at the other

Your friends see a shape draped in a white shroud in dim light. You explain that this is the infamous "growing ghost" of Tom Ladshaw. Tom Ladshaw was a retired explosives expert for the army who used to live in the swamps of Louisiana. He came to your town to visit some relatives and died a horrible death when his shirt caught on one car bumper and his pants caught on another. Poor Mr. Ladshaw was stretched to death. As you say these words, the white shape begins to moan, and then right before eveyone's eyes, it stretches up toward the ceiling and grows to be 8 feet tall. Then just as suddenly, it shrinks down to about 3 feet high. The lights dim, and you lead the spirit tour onward.

*How You Do It*

Your assistant holds the stick, with the inside of the bowl glued or tacked to one end of it, so that the bottom of the bowl is uppermost, at about eye level. Drape the tube of cloth over your assistant and the bowl so that he or she looks like a ghost.

Your assistant kneels down. When the group comes by, the assistant should moan and shake a little, then slowly stand up and simply raise the stick over his or her head. When your assistant's arms are stretched as high as possible, the "ghost" will be about 8 feet tall! One thing to remember: Make sure there is no backlighting, or your audience will see the outline of your assistant through the cloth.

## THE HEADLESS MAN

*What You'll Need*

One long overcoat
One full mask of a man's head stuffed with newspaper
One rubber knife

Lead your audience toward a dark corner. Suddenly, a dim light comes on, and they see before them a headless man. In one hand, he holds his head, and in the other, he holds a knife. "Help me," he moans. "Please help me!"

*How You Do It*

This is a snap. Your assistant wears the overcoat buttoned up over his head. Use newspaper for extra padding to fill out the shoulders. His arms go into the sleeves. Your assistant holds the mask in the crook of one arm and the rubber knife in the other. After peeking out to make sure you're ready, you can both scare the heck out of your friends!

## THE DEAD LIVE AGAIN

*What You'll Need*

One large cardboard box, the kind refrigerators are shipped in
Enough material to line the box
Scary makeup, either bought from a kit or homemade

Lead your group into another corner where a coffin is displayed. When they look inside, they'll see a dead body! To the accompaniment of spooky music, explain to them that the man died just this morning and the funeral will be tomorrow. Suddenly, as you're speaking, one of the dead man's hands begins to twitch, and right before their eyes, tries to grab a member of the audience!

*How You Do It*

Cut down the box to the approximate shape of a coffin. (You may need an adult to help you with this.) Line it with material to make it comfortable. Decorate it to look like a coffin. Make up your assistant to look like a dead person, and you're ready to stage his awakening!

## THE FIVE-FINGERED HAND

*What You'll Need*

One small wooden or cardboard box with a hinged lid and no bottom
One large cardboard box, the kind refrigerators are packed in
One tablecloth or sheet
One piece of candy

Tell your friends that you have in your possession the dreaded five-fingered hand, which you've borrowed from a museum. Show them the box, which should be resting on top of a table covered with the tablecloth. Put a piece of candy down next to the box. To their horror, the hand will lift the lid of the box, grab the candy, and pop back inside!

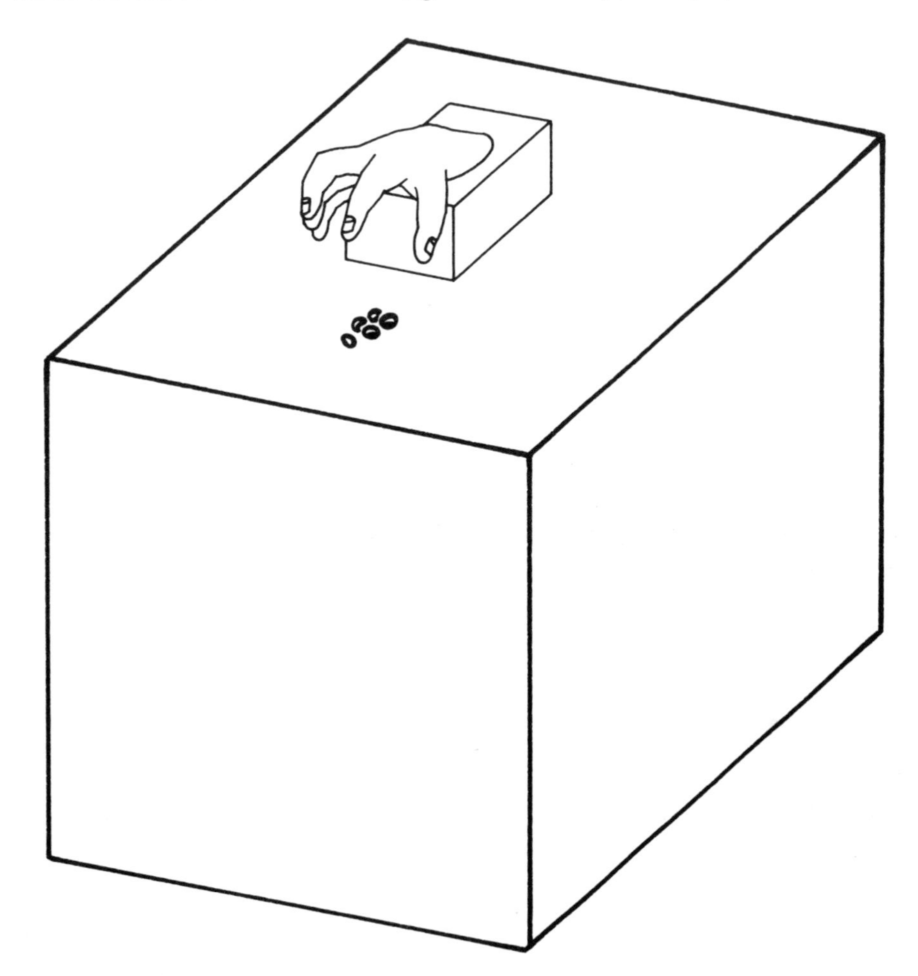

*How You Do It*

Cut the large box down so that it's about 3 feet high. Cut a hole about 6 inches round in the top. (Ask an adult to help with all the cutting.) Drape the tablecloth over the large box. Cut a hole through the cloth (make sure your mother doesn't need this one anymore!) and line it up with the hole in the box. Place the smaller box directly over the hole. If you want to, make up your assistant's hand so that it looks as frightening as possible. Put the candy on the table next to the box. Your assistant will climb inside the big box, reach up through the hole, open the small box lid, grab the candy, and pull his or her hand back.

## THE GHOST'S CORNER

*What You'll Need*

One brick
One picture, hung on the wall
One tin or plastic cup
One table
Heavy black thread
A tablecloth your mother no longer needs

Lead your audience toward the final frightening tableau. They see a table set against a wall with some objects on it. As spooky music plays in the background, some very strange things start happening: a brick falls off the table—by itself. A picture hanging on the wall suddenly goes crooked. A cup moves to the end of the table and falls off. A door behind the table slams—all by itself!

*How You Do It*

The objects that seem to move by themselves are actually controlled by your assistant. He's under the table, hidden by the cloth. You will attach a piece of heavy black thread to each object. Pull the end of each piece of string through a small hole in the tablecloth. The strings are attached to the objects to be moved. The assistant will pull on these hidden threads to make the objects move.

# SOUND AND TOUCH EFFECTS

## SOUND EFFECTS

We talked about sound effects earlier, when we told you how to tell a ghost story. Here's how to make some spooky sound effects. Scary sounds help create the proper atmosphere as your guests walk slowly through your haunted house.

- Screams are among the most chilling sounds you can use, and they require no special equipment. A couple of noisy friends will do the trick!
- Party blowouts—the things that unroll and make a loud noise when you blow through the mouthpiece—are wonderful, especially in the dark. They have the bonus of being a visual effect, too, if you cover them with luminous paint.
- Pennies dropped onto small pieces of dry ice make a deliciously spine-tingling shriek as the metal contracts from touching the dry ice. But be very careful—the dry ice can burn you. *Note: Make sure you talk to your parents about this one before you plan on doing it.*
- Attach long crepe-paper streamers to the front of a fan. As your guests go by, turn it off and on. This produces a creepy, shivery sound. If it's close enough, the streamers will brush against your guests, along with a chilly blast from the fan. Ask your parents to supervise you while you do this trick because fans can be dangerous if your fingers get into the blades.

- Rattling chains is another old standard of ghost tales. You can buy "chains" at a local novelty store, magic shop, or hardware store.
- You can use a tape recorder to make a wide range of noises. Clanking, moaning, ominous thuds, knives being scraped along metal—the list of possibilities is endless.

Here's an effect that depends on a combination of sound and light. Paint a pair of rubber gloves and a rubber knife with luminous paint. At the appropriate moment, have your assistant, wearing the gloves, pull the knife out of a bag. Only his hands and the rubber knife will be visible in the dark. Have him raise the rubber knife high and, with a loud scream, dramatically bring it down. *Note: Do not touch people with the knife, because they might try to defend themselves.*

## TOUCHY FEELY EFFECTS

"Touchy feely" effects are scary because they involve some objects that brush against your audience. Like the other effects, they depend heavily on the audience's imagination for their success or failure. The atmosphere you create is also important.

- *Jungle worms.* You can introduce effects with an anecdote: "Twenty years ago, one of the children who lived on this block traveled to Africa and brought home a pair of African jungle worms, which are very rare and poisonous. Somehow the worms escaped and bred. Now hundreds of them live in the sewers under this block. Every year at just about this time they come out of the sewers to perform a primitive mating dance. Sometimes they get into a house through the basement, and when that happens—oh, no! Here they come!" At this point, your friends feel a whole squad of jungle worms landing on their heads and shoulders. (You can make jungle worms out of partially cooked spaghetti.) Finish your ghoulish tale by leaning over the nearest guest, picking a worm off her head, and popping it into your mouth!

JUNGLE WORMS

- "This house has always been plagued by enormous spiders," you say as you lead your guests into the next room of your haunted house. "Some of these spiders spin giant floor-to-ceiling webs." As your guests pass into the next room, giant spiderwebs will brush their faces. You can make these "webs" by taping or tacking a rope across the top of the doorway. Tie dozens of pieces of long, fine thread to the rope and let them hang down into the doorway, to about 4 feet from the ground. Your guests won't be able to see the threads in the dark, but they *will* be able to feel them!

- Have your assistant soak a cotton glove in cold water. Have him wring it out thoroughly so that it's damp but not dripping wet and put it on his hand. Then have the assistant glide past your guests in the dark, placing a cold, clammy hand on each of them.

SPIDERWEBS—use dark thread

# TRICKS, EFFECTS, AND MAGICAL ILLUSIONS

On the following pages, you will find all kinds of tricks, illusions, and effects that you can use to boggle the minds of your willing victims. Some of these effects are simple, some are complicated, but all of them depend on your acting skill. Remember, no matter how simple something seems to you once you know how it's done, to your audience the tricks will be amazing, and your friends will think you are a gifted magician.

To help you with some of the following tricks, we've created a key to let you know how much advance preparation each trick requires. An asterisk * before a trick tells you that some advance preparation is required. A double asterisk ** indicates that a lot of advance preparation is required and that this is a more advanced trick.

## LUMINOUS EFFECTS

You can do many tricks with a little paint—luminous paint, that is. You can buy luminous paint at magic shops and at some five-and-tens. (If you have trouble finding it, see the list of suppliers at the back of this book.) Handling the paint properly is the key to making these effects work. You must paint the object you'll be using and store it immediately in a dark bag or room. *Make sure it is stored where no light can reach it.* About ten or twenty minutes before you're ready to use the object, expose it to strong light for about one minute—a 100-watt light bulb will do nicely.

Put the object back in the dark bag or room until you're ready to use it. The glow will last for about twenty minutes.

Objects painted with luminous paint have lots of scare value, especially when you whisk them out of nowhere, i.e., the black prop bag described in "holding a seance" (page 80). Remember, *you* know how it's done, but your victims—we mean, your audience—don't, so play it for all it's worth!

*Note*: All luminous effects require a dark room.

## * FLOATING EYES

*What You'll Need*

Luminous paint
One pair of dark shoes

Your guests walk through a dark room which, you inform them, is visited from time to time by ghosts. Some of the ghosts are friendly, some not so friendly. Suddenly, you grab a guest by the elbow. "Look!" you shout. A pair of ghostly eyes appear mysteriously near the floor and float upward. Just as suddenly, they disappear!

*How You Do It*

You will need a helper wearing dark shoes for this trick. You prepare for this by painting a pair of large, scary eyes on the sole of each shoe, using luminous paint. Store the shoes in a dark room until you're ready to use them, and expose them to strong light for one minute before you do the trick. (Don't walk in mud, rain, or dirt before you perform this trick.) When you grab your friend's elbow and point, your helper will raise one foot slowly off the floor so that the eyes are exposed!

## * MR. BONE-JANGLES

*What You'll Need*

Luminous paint
One sheet of cardboard 5 or 6 feet long

In your darkened room, while your guests are still recovering from the ghostly eyes, you can make their hair stand on end by pointing to anoth-

FLOATING EYES

er corner of the room where, as if by magic, a glowing skeleton suddenly appears!

*How You Do It*

To prepare for this trick, cover a skeleton with luminous paint or paint a ghostly figure on a piece of cardboard and tape it to the inside of a closed door. When the time is right, quickly open the door and expose the glowing skeleton.

## * THE BOUNCING GHOST

*What You'll Need*

Luminous paint
One beach ball

While your guests are in the dark room, you can make glowing spots materialize from thin air and bounce around the room.

*How You Do It*

Paint luminous dots on the ball. Expose the ball to strong light and then store it in a dark place. When you're ready, have your assistant bounce the ball around the room in the dark. Pretty soon everyone will be bouncing it. For greater effect, cover the tapping of the bouncing ball with scary sound effects such as loud moaning or rattling chains.

## * THE INFLATABLE GHOST

*What You'll Need*

Luminous paint
One balloon

"Oh, my gosh!" you scream while leading your victims through the darkened room. "There's a ghost materializing from nowhere!" You point to a corner of the room where, before their eyes, a small glowing face gets larger and larger until, with a large bang, it suddenly disappears.

*How You Do It*

Paint a luminous face on an inflated balloon. Then carefully let the air out of the balloon and store it in a dark place. When the time comes, you or your assistant will blow up the balloon—and a glowing face will appear as if out of thin air. *Note:* You might want to use sound effects to mask the sounds of blowing up the balloon. Rattling chains would be effective here.

## * THE GHOSTLY SNAKE

*What You'll Need*

Luminous paint
Two narrow 20-inch strips of white gauze

"Many years ago," you say to your friends in the pitch-dark room, "the children in this house had two pet rattlesnakes. The snakes escaped one night, bit everyone in the family, and then crept away underground when all the people were dead. But every once in a while they come back and . . . oh, no! There they are!" Your horrified audience turns to see two glowing snakes wriggling across the floor!

*How You Do It*

Cover the two strips of gauze with luminous paint, or dip them into the can of paint so that you don't miss any spots. At the right moment, have your assistant slowly draw the strips out of the dark storage place and pull them across the floor while another helper shakes a child's rattle or a bag of stones.

## * THE WRITING ON THE WALL

*What You'll Need*

Luminous paint
Two sheets of cardboard, about 2 feet by 2 feet
One small paintbrush
Electrician's tape

"You know," you tell your audience in the darkened room, "every once in a while the spirits get lonely. When that happens, they like to send messages to us from the spirit world. If I concentrate very hard, I can get one of them to do that. Would you like to see?"

Put your hands to your forehead and mumble an unintelligible spell. "Close your eyes to help me concentrate," you tell your guests. But whether they do or not, they'll be shocked to see a glowing message suddenly appear on the wall of the dark room.

*How You Do It*

Using luminous paint, write a message on a piece of cardboard and tape it to one wall of the room. To make it interesting, write something to or about one of the people who will be at the party. Remember to expose the cardboard to strong light for one minute and then store it in a dark place until you're ready to use it. The glow will last for about twenty minutes. Tape a piece of plain black cardboard over the message with two pieces of electrician's tape, one at the top and the other at the bottom. At the appropriate moment, have your assistant peel away the top piece of tape and let the cardboard drop down so that the message is exposed.

## * RADIOACTIVE FALLOUT

*What You'll Need*

Luminous paint
Popcorn (popped)
Several narrow strips of paper 6 inches long

"You know," you tell your guests, "one of the people who used to live in this house was a nuclear physicist who helped develop the atom bomb. Every once in a while now, some strange glowing stuff appears in this room, sort of like radioactive fallout. Do you think it could be connected to the nuclear physicist?" As your guests figure this out, you suddenly point. "Look, there it is!" Sure enough, little crackling bits of glowing matter suddenly start raining from the ceiling and walls.

*How You Do It*

Dip the popcorn and the strips of paper into a can of luminous paint. Let the paint dry. Crumple the paper. Expose all of the materials to strong light and store them in a dark bag. At the right time have your assistant take the popcorn and paper strips out of the bag and toss them at the audience. If your assistant stands on a short stepladder, the fallout will appear to be raining down on them.

## * ACID RAIN

*What You'll Need*

Luminous paint
Uncooked rice

"We're doing some pretty terrible things to this planet," you say to your guests. "The Indians used to think that one day the earth would revolt and have its revenge on us. As a matter of fact, an Indian family lived right on this very spot many years before the Europeans came here.

Good thing they never stuck around to hear about acid rain." Suddenly, glowing bits of matter start dropping from the ceiling. "Oh, no!" you cry, "maybe they have!"

*How You Do It*

Soak the uncooked rice in luminous paint, let it dry, expose to light, store, and have your assistant throw the rice on your guests at the crucial moment.

## NUCLEAR CRAWLERS

*What You'll Need*

- Luminous paint
- One plastic spider or other bug with a squeeze-bulb attachment to make it move

You can do this trick right after the radioactive fallout effect. "Sometimes this whole area is covered with radioactive stuff," you say while your friends are still clutching each other in the dark. "I wonder what happens to all the animals and bugs that are exposed to it?" Your answer suddenly comes crawling across the floor. "It's a nuclear crawler!"

*How You Do It*

At a toy store or novelty shop, you can buy a plastic spider or insect that will move when you press a bulb attached to a tube that is fastened to its body. Simply paint the toy with luminous paint and unveil it at the right time. It will hop across the room and strike terror into the hearts of even your bravest friends!

## * STAGE BLOOD

*Note: Ask your parents before you use stage blood.* Stage blood can be very messy and can stain your clothing and the room you are working in. It's best if you do this with a grown-up around, and you should do the mixing in a sink. Here are two good ways to make stage blood:

- Mix clear corn syrup with red food coloring. Pour the two into a bottle and shake it. Add more coloring or more syrup until you have a mixture that is the right consistency and color. This is the most real-looking stage blood you can make at home.
- Mix red water-color paint with a little water. Add more water or more paint until you get the proper consistency and color.

If you don't want to make the mixture at home, you can purchase stage blood from a magic shop or from one of the suppliers listed at the back of this book.

## * THE PIERCED ARM

*What You'll Need*

One thin plastic straw
Rubber cement
Stage blood (optional)

You can do this trick safely and simply while you're telling a scary story, preferably one that includes a malicious ghost with a taste for revenge. Slowly roll up your sleeve and show the audience an ordinary soda straw that seems to pierce the skin of your arm.

*How You Do It*

Coat a patch of skin on the inside of your forearm with rubber cement. Lay the straw across the cement-treated area. Pinch your skin together over the straw; the skin will stick together, creating the illusion that the straw is under your skin. For added fright value, spill a little stage blood down your arm and let it dry before you put your cape or jacket on.

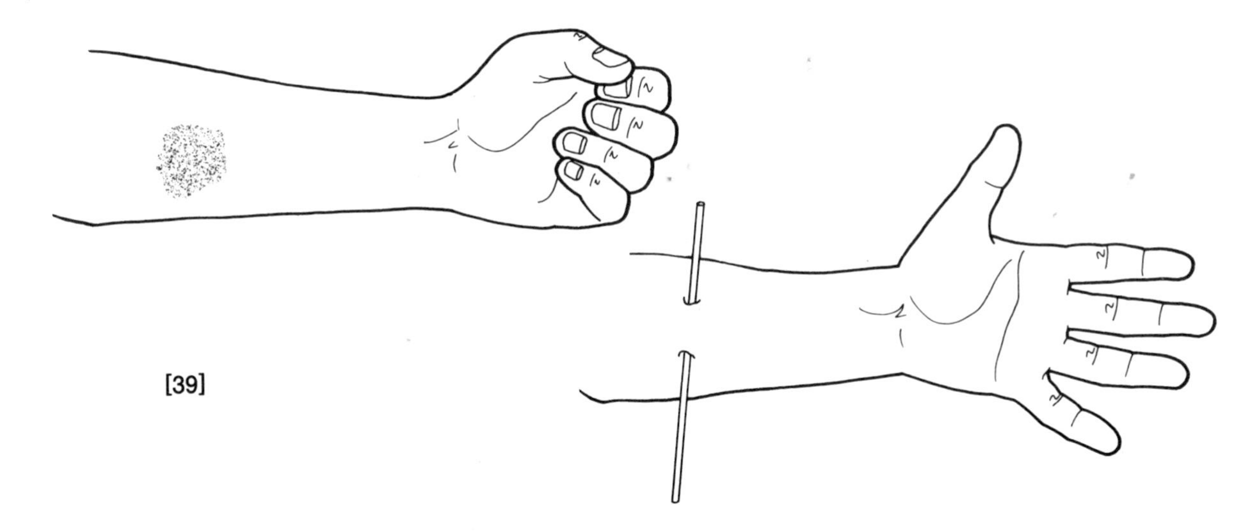

To remove the straw and cement, simply pull the straw through and rub the skin of your forearm. The dry cement will rub right off.

*Note:* Some people are allergic to rubber cement. Find out whether you're one of them before you attempt this illusion. You can do this by painting a little rubber cement over a patch of skin—the inside of your elbow is a good place—and letting it dry and remain there for several hours. If your skin doesn't redden, swell, or show other signs of allergic reaction, you shouldn't have any problem. If it does, just remove the cement and avoid illusions that require its application. It will also help if you shave off the hair on the part of your arm where you will apply rubber cement. If you don't, you may pull out a bunch of arm hair when you rub the rubber cement to remove it—and that would be truly painful.

## * SCARFACE

Here are two ways to make realistic, frightening scars on your face and body.

- Buy some rigid collodion at a specialty store or makeup shop. Paint a one-inch collodion "scar" on your face and let the glue dry. As it dries, it will pucker your skin in a very realistic and gruesome way. If you add another coat it will look even better. You can remove the liquid collodion with cold cream or makeup remover. Then wash your face with soap and water.
- Paint a line of rubber cement on your face and let it dry. (Make sure before you try this that you aren't allergic to rubber cement; see the pierced arm trick, page 39.) Pinch your skin together after the glue is dry, and it will look like a scar. If you want an even more ghoulish effect, dip a small paintbrush—the kind used to paint model cars and trains—into some stage blood and apply it sparingly to the "scar." You can rub the cement off with your fingers when you want to get rid of your scar.

## * THE SLASHING KNIFE

*What You'll Need*

One rubber knife
Stage blood
One eyedropper or nosedropper

SCARFACE—using rubber cement

*How You Do It*

Fill the bulb or the dropper with stage blood. Tape it carefully to one side of the rubber knife blade. Hold your wrist up, facing your friends. Run the rubber knife blade across your wrist, with the bulb side facing you, and squeeze the bulb. A line of stage blood will appear across your wrist. Don't try this illusion at the dinner table or over your parents' good carpeting. Even if your friends notice that it's a rubber knife, they'll still wonder how you did it!

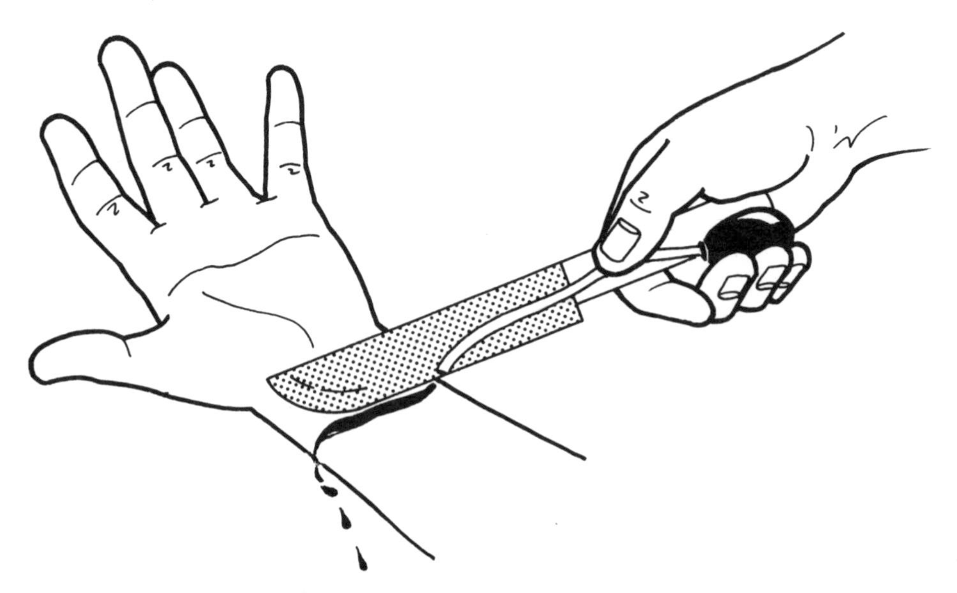

## * THE DIRTY TOWEL

*What You'll Need*

Two clean *old* towels, preferably white (check to make sure your parents won't mind if you ruin them)
Paint or ink (enough to make several dirty handprints)
One sewing needle
Sewing thread that matches the towels

Introduce this illusion with the following speech: "There's a ghost in this room. I can feel its presence. This ghost likes to roll around in the ectoplasmic mud. And I'm going to prove that it's here." Hold up the towels and show your guests both sides. "I'm going to ask all of you to wipe your hands on these towels," you announce. "The ghost has touched one, and only one, of you. That person's hands will leave dirty handprints on the towel.'' Sure enough, when you pass around the towel, someone's hands leave muddy prints!

*How You Do It*

For this effect, one towel should be smaller than the other one. If your towels are the same size, you'll have to cut one in half. Sew the half-size towel to the middle of the bigger towel so that it forms a flap. Now rub your hands in the mud or dirt, and make dirty handprints on one side of the half-size towel. (Don't forget to wash up right away, or you'll leave handprints on other things too!)

When you first hold the towel up to the audience, you hold the extra piece up, too, so it's hidden from sight (see illustration). After someone wipes his or her hands on the towel, quickly turn the towel as you hold it up and let the extra piece—with the dirty handprints on it—drop down and be seen. Practice this in front of a mirror until you can do it so smoothly that even your parents won't be able to tell how you did it!

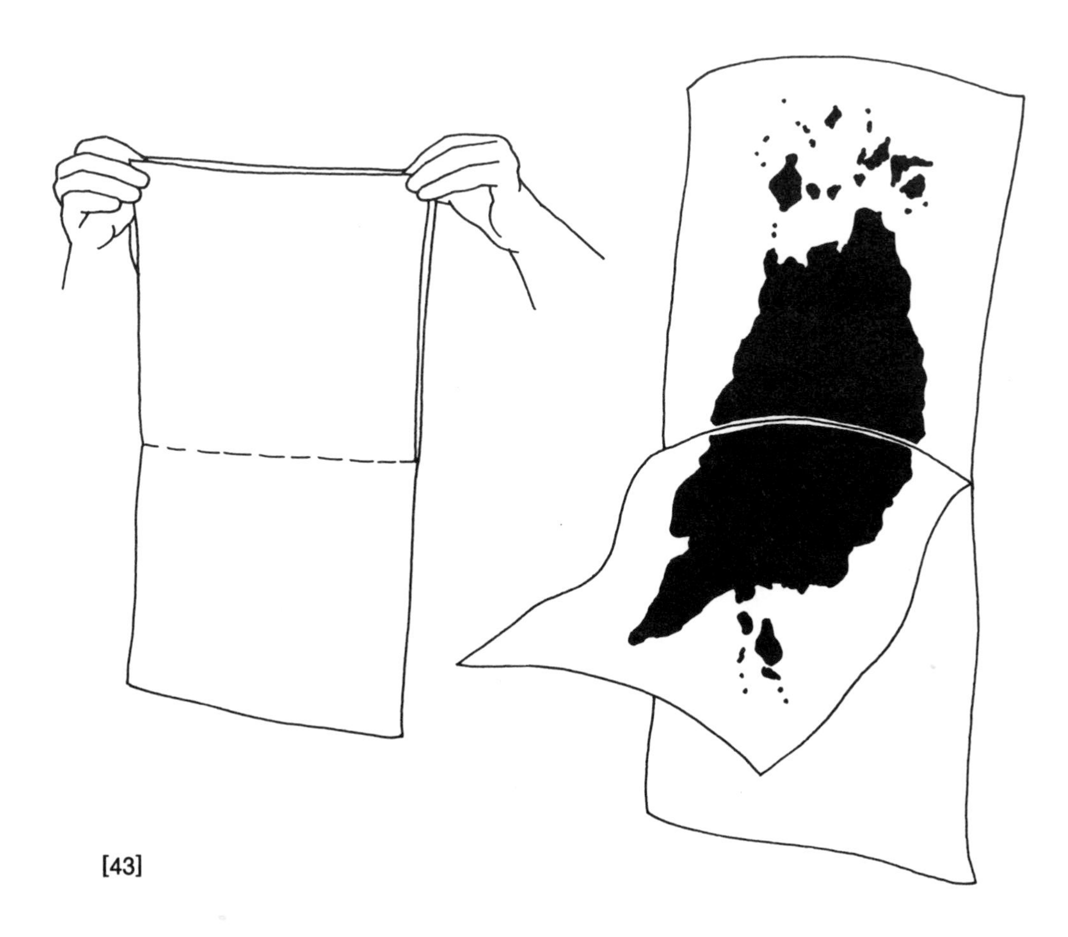

## * THE SEVERED HAND

*What You'll Need*

Fake rubber hand
Rubber knife
A long-sleeved shirt or blouse

*How You Do It*

Pull your hand up inside your sleeve and hold the fake hand out as if it were your own. (Remember to match the correct hand with the correct arm!) Use your other hand to slash at your wrist with the rubber knife until the fake hand falls off. (After all, a rubber knife should cut a rubber hand.) Do this with the lights dimmed and have your assistant turn off the lights just as the hand falls off.

* THE FLOATING SKULL

*What You'll Need*

Plastic skull
(available at novelty stores)
Scissors

*How You Do It*

Ask an adult to help you cut a star-shaped hole about one inch wide in the back of the skull. Just before you're ready to perform, insert your thumb into the hole up to the first joint. If you do this correctly, the skull should be wedged onto your thumb. Put the fingers of both your hands around the skull and lift it off a table. Slowly remove your fingers but not your thumb. The skull will appear to be floating in the air! Practice this illusion in front of a mirror before trying it on your friends.

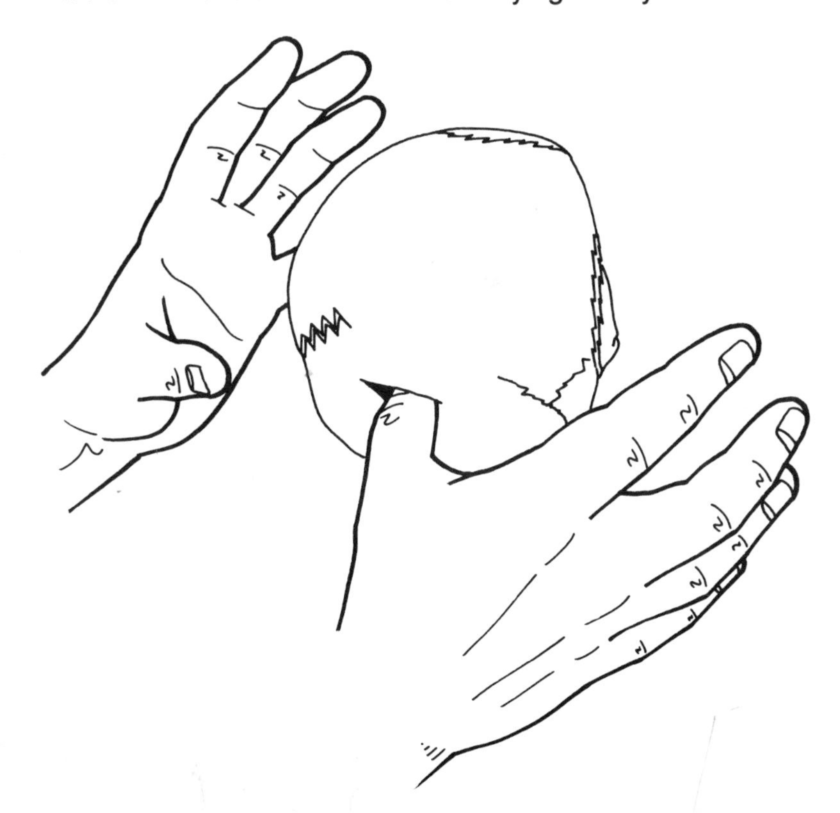

## * SCAREDY PEPPER

*What You'll Need*

Bowl of water
Black pepper
Bar of soap

"My brother brought this pepper back from the Caribbean," you tell your audience. "Down there they practice witchcraft. This pepper can sense the presence of a spirit and run away from it!" Shake some of the pepper onto the surface of the water in the bowl. Reach into the air, pretend to grab a spirit in your hand—you can fake a struggle at this point to make it realistic—and put your index finger into the water at the edge of the bowl. The pepper will seem to run away from your hand!

*How You Do It*

Before doing this trick, scrape your fingernail along a bar of soap and trap some of the soap under your nail. Don't clean it out. When you put that same finger into the bowl of water, the soap will change the surface tension of the water and cause the pepper to "run away" from your finger.

## * THE MUMMY'S FINGER

*What You'll Need*

One earring box or other small jewelry box
Cotton packing

"I found this box in an antiques store," you tell your audience. "The woman who owned the store told me it was from Rumania. I told her I wanted to buy it, but she said it would be bad luck for her to sell it, so she gave it to me instead. It belonged to a three-thousand-year-old mummy. It looks almost real, as you'll see." You open the box. "Go on," you say, "touch it." When someone from the audience touches it, the finger moves! If you do it well, they'll scream.

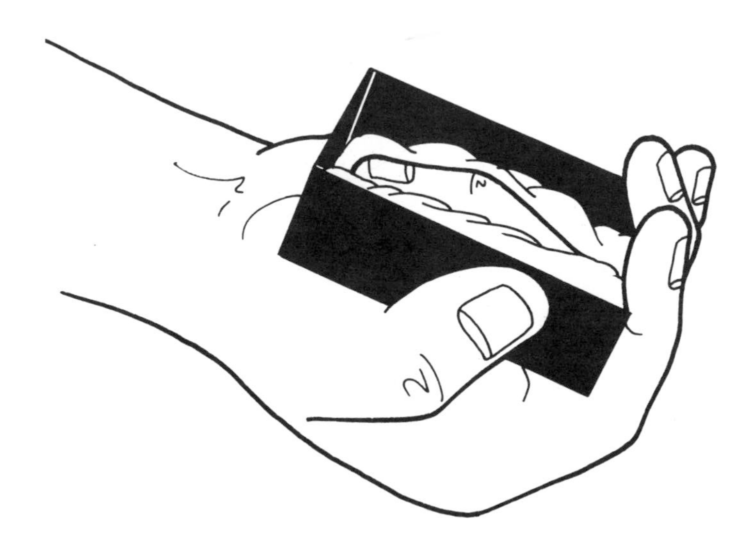

*How You Do It*

Carefully cut a hole in the bottom of the box through which your middle finger will fit. Lay some cotton in the bottom of the box, insert your finger through the hole, and put the lid on. When you hold the box in the palm of your hand, no one will notice that your finger is missing. When your friends open the box and touch the finger, wiggle it very slightly. You'll be surprised at how effective this trick can be—you might even believe it yourself!

## * A DAYLIGHT SÉANCE

*What You'll Need*

Yardstick
A piece of black cloth, approximately 3 feet by 3 feet
Two pairs of wrist-length white gloves
A handful of cotton balls
A small rubber ball, a candle, a whistle, a piece of fruit,
a deck of cards—or other similar props

Place several props on the table before you: a candle, a deck of playing cards, a piece of fruit, a rubber ball, a whistle. Hold the black cloth in front of you with both hands. Your friends will be amazed to see the objects fly up under the cloth and do strange things, all while you continue to hold the curtain with both hands!!

*How You Do It*

Stuff one right-hand glove with cotton so it looks like there is a real hand inside it. Glue that glove to the right side of the yardstick above the curtain, to the place where your right hand would be if you were actually holding the prop with both hands. When you perform the trick, wear the other pair of gloves. Raise the curtain with both hands and then remove your right hand. The audience still sees two hands holding the curtain! Now your right hand is free to pick objects up behind the curtain and make them fly about. You can use your imagination and dexterity to make a ball fly out at the audience, a candle dance in the air. And if you raise the curtain up for a moment so that it covers your mouth, you can make the whistle "blow," too!

## * THE BLOODY FLYSWATTER

*What You'll Need*

Ordinary flyswatter (the kind with a long plastic handle)
Stage blood
One plastic tube as long as the handle of the flyswatter
(look for tubing in an aquarium supply store)
One small eyedropper or plastic bulb
One small plastic fly

*How You Do It*

Tape or glue the plastic tube to the length of the flyswatter handle. Attach the bulb at the bottom end, and make sure the tube is inserted into the bulb. Fill the bulb with stage blood. Swat at an invisible fly or a friend without squeezing the bulb. Then you can announce, "I've got it!" and swing at the plastic fly, squeezing the bulb. "Blood" will squirt from the flyswatter! Note: remember that stage blood will stain walls and clothing, so it might be best to "swat" the fly on an old newspaper that can then be thrown away.

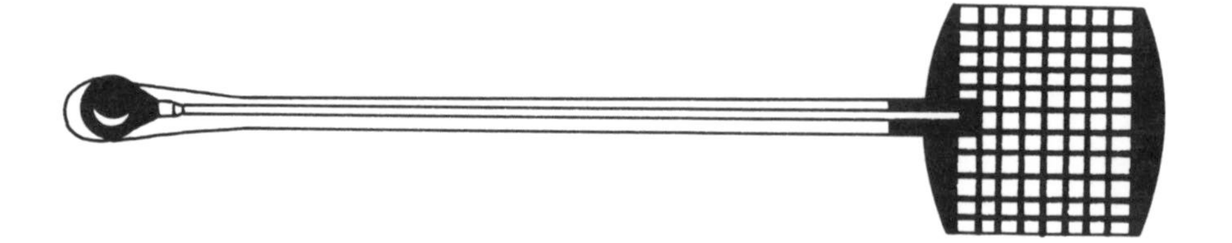

## THE HYPNOTIZED BALL I

*What You'll Need*

One Ping-Pong ball
One table

Tell your friends that, before their very eyes, you will hypnotize a Ping-Pong ball and command it to move from one side of a table to another. You wave your hands around in the air, make some mysterious "hypnotizing" motions, lean over the table, and the ball will start to move over the tabletop.

*How You Do It*

This trick is simple, but it's guaranteed to fool even the most skeptical of your friends. As you lean over the tabletop, mumbling magic words, simply purse your lips slightly and blow at the point where the ball touches the tabletop. If you can keep your audience looking at your hands, they'll never notice what your lips are doing. Make sure you blow silently. Practice this one before you try it on an audience.

## * THE HYPNOTIZED BALL II

*What You'll Need*

- Ping-Pong ball
- Table
- Tablecloth
- Curtain ring (available at a five-and-ten)
- A piece of string a few inches longer than the tablecloth

*How You Do It*

This trick is guaranteed to convince the skeptics who thought they saw you blowing the Ping-Pong ball in the previous trick. Tie one end of the string to the curtain ring. Place the ring on the table across from where you will be sitting and stretch the string across the table so that it hangs over the edge in front of you. Carefully spread out the tablecloth so that it hides the ring. Make sure you can see your end of the string, so that you can grab it when it's time to do the trick.

Tell your friends you're going to prove that the Ping-Pong ball is hypnotized. Place the ball across the table from you. Be sure it's sitting inside the ring. Make more mystic passes with your hands. Meanwhile, pull gently on the string hanging down underneath your side of the tablecloth. The ball will slowly move across the table at your command! Make sure you pull the string slowly and steadily so that the ball doesn't roll out of the ring.

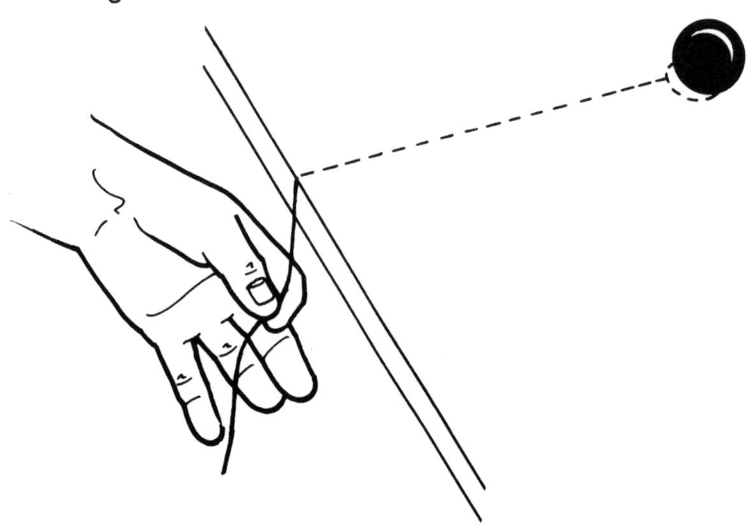

## * THE BALL THAT WALKS A TIGHTROPE

*What You'll Need*

- A piece of yarn about 15 inches long
- A piece of white thread with a large knot tied in each end, exactly 15 inches long with the knots tied in it.
- A Ping-Pong ball
- A table

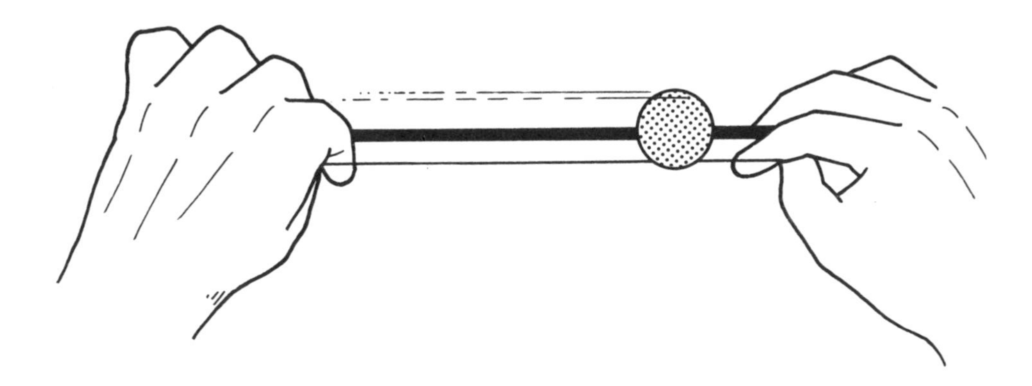

To prepare your audience for this trick, tell them the story of the famous tightrope walker, Philippe Petit, who stretched a rope between the twin towers of the World Trade Center in New York City and walked across it to safety. Then bring out the Ping-Pong ball and tell everyone that it contains the spirit of another famous tightrope walker, Charles Blondin, who walked across Niagara Falls on a tightrope many years before Petit was born.

Next put the yarn on the table and stretch it out straight in front of the ball. Try to balance the ball on the yarn and fail. Then say the magic words, "Mumbo jumbo, walk the rope," pick up one end of the yarn in each hand and stretch it out in the air. The ball will be balanced on the yarn! It will even roll from one end to the other until you command it to fall, at which point it will drop to the table.

*How You Do It*

To prepare this trick, tie or glue the ends of the thread to the ends of the yarn. Pick up the yarn so that one finger at either end rests between the yarn and the thread. Now you can balance the ball *between* the yarn and the thread and even roll it up and down. When you want it to fall, just let the yarn go slack. Practice this so you don't fumble with the thread too much while getting it in place.

## * THE BALANCING BALL

*What You'll Need*

Ping-Pong ball
Rubber cement

Put the ball away after you finish doing the tightrope trick. Say to your friends, "Oh, I forgot! Here's another trick I think you'll like." Pull out the Ping-Pong ball. "My great-great-grandmother was a mermaid," you tell your audience, "and to prove it, I'll show you that I can catch this ball on the end of my nose like a seal." Throw the ball up in the air, catch it on the end of your nose, and it will stay there! Balance it for a few moments—you might even want to twirl around—and then snatch it from your nose and take a deep bow!

*How You Do It*

This trick is simple. You will pull out a second Ping-Pong ball—not the one you used in the tightrope trick. This one will be covered with a thin coat of rubber cement which should be fully dry. Before you start your performance, you will paint your nose with rubber cement as well, from the bridge to the tip. No one will be able to see the cement, as it is transparent when it's dry.

All you have to do is catch the ball on your nose. The cement will make it stick to your nose. All you need now is good showmanship!

## * THE THIRSTY GHOST

*What You'll Need*

Plate lifter
Tablecloth
Glass half filled with soda

"You all know by now that this house is haunted," you say to your audience. "But did you know that it's haunted by a thirsty ghost?" You place the glass on the table. Before everyone's eyes, the glass starts to bounce up and down with no living person touching it!

*How You Do It*

A plate lifter (available at any novelty store) is a plastic or rubber bladder with a long plastic tube leading to a rubber squeeze bulb. You prepare for this trick by setting the plate lifter on the table and then covering the table, the lifter, and the tube with a tablecloth. Be sure the tube is not noticeable to your audience and the bulb is near your hand. Set the glass down on top of the bladder of the plate lifter. When you secretly squeeze the bulb, the glass will move!

BALANCING BALL

## THE DETACHABLE INDEX FINGER

"I was once bitten by a vampire," you tell your friends. "But because I was protected by a spell, the only effect it had on me is that I can pull my finger off. Watch!" As your friends look on, you calmly reach over with one hand and pull your index finger off at the joint!

*How You Do It*

This trick is really an illusion. If you do it properly, you will fool your friends every time. Hold your left hand in front of your body, palm toward you, with the thumb up. Bend your index finger in. Now bend the thumb of your right hand into the palm. Hold the thumb of your right hand where the index finger of your left hand would be. Cover the joint with your right index finger. This will require practice in front of a mirror, but it's worth every second. Now slowly slide your right hand away from your left hand, keeping your right thumb on top of your left middle finger. If you do it smoothly and correctly, it will really look as if you've detached your left index finger. Boy, can you scare Mom and Dad with this one!

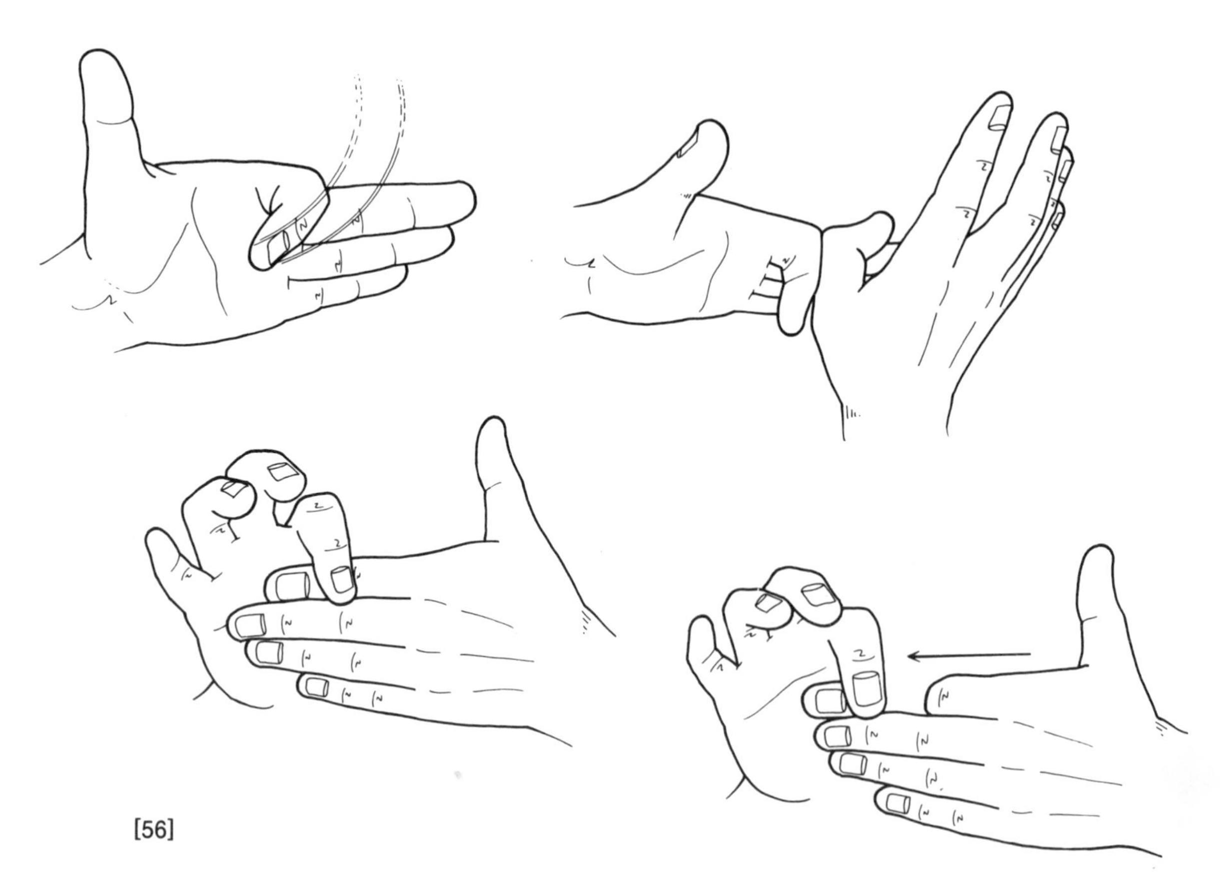

## THE INVINCIBLE THUMB

*What You'll Need*

- Handkerchief
- Raw carrot about the size of your thumb
- 4 or 5 straight pins

"An Eastern mystic in Tibet taught me how to endure pain," you tell your friends. "And now I'm going to prove it to you!" Hold up a handkerchief and have one of your friends examine it to make sure it's ordinary. Drape it over your thumb. Have your mother or father stick pins into your thumb. Keep a smile on your face as you show your friends that you can endure pain!

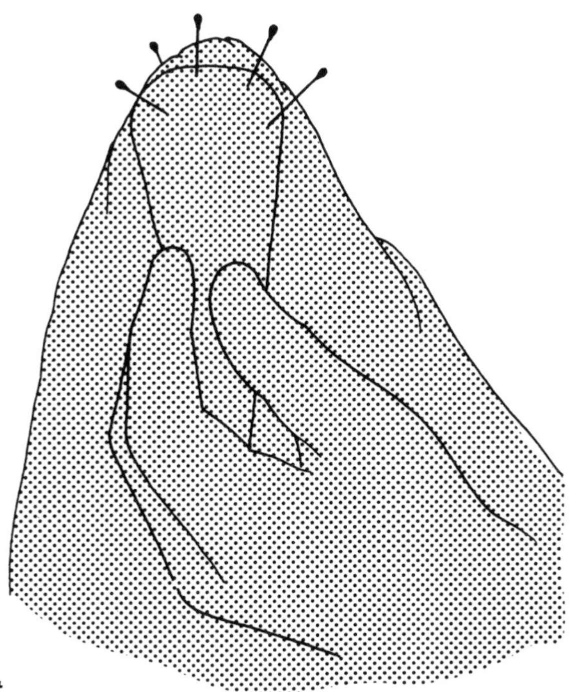

*How You Do It*

To perform this, palm the carrot. Now pretend to drape the handkerchief over your thumb, but you'll really drape it over the carrot. The pins, of course, go into the carrot. As you pull the handkerchief away, palm the carrot again and slip it into your pocket. It's simple, after a little practice in palming the carrot, and it works every time! Note: Be careful that you don't get carried away and jab yourself with a pin. That's not part of the trick.

## * STOPPING YOUR PULSE

*What You'll Need*

Handkerchief or bandanna

"That Eastern mystic also taught me how to control my body in other ways," you tell your friends. "In fact, I can even stop my own pulse for a little while!" Hold your wrist out so a friend from the audience can feel your pulse. (Remember to tell the person not to use his or her thumb, as it has a pulse of its own.) Grit your teeth; concentrate. Your friend will be amazed to feel your pulse actually slow down and stop!

*How You Do It*

You are actually going to stop the pulse in your wrist for a few moments in this trick. Roll a handkerchief or ball of cloth up and place it in the armpit of the arm you'll hold out to your friend. When you want to stop your pulse, squeeze your arm against your body, pressing the cloth in deeply. If the cloth is in the right position, the pulse in that arm will indeed stop for a few moments. The cloth presses against a pressure point that controls the flow of blood through a major artery.

*Note:* be sure not to do this trick for more than ten seconds at a time or too often.

## * VAMPIRE TWINE

*What You'll Need*

A 2-foot length of twine, preferably butcher's twine, the kind that is made up of separate strands twisted together
Rubber cement or white glue
Scissors

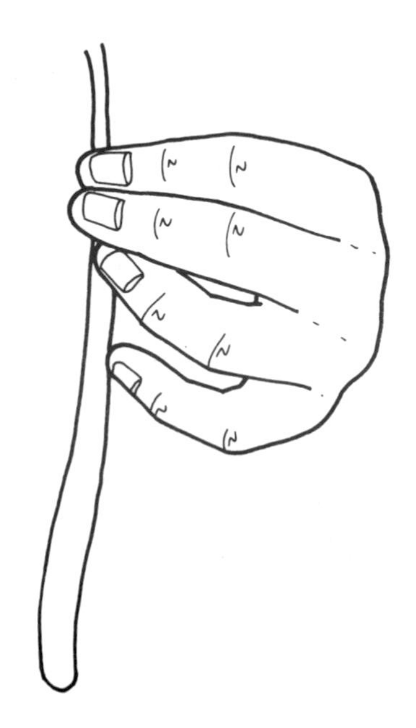

"This twine came from a vampire's coffin in Transylvania," you say to your audience, holding up an ordinary-looking piece of twine. "I know it's true because this piece of twine is indestructible. And I'm going to prove it to you right now by cutting it apart and then restoring it!"

*How You Do It*

Separate the strands at the center of the length of twine into two equal groups of strands. Twist each group of strands so that they appear to be ends. These "ends" should be 1 or 2 inches long. Now take the *real* ends and lightly glue or cement them together. When they dry, it will look like an ordinary piece of twine, except that what looks like the middle is really the ends glued together, and the "ends" are really the middle! Now hold the twine up by the "ends"—really the middle—with the joined ends hanging down. Have a friend hold them while you cut them away. It should now appear that you are holding two separate pieces of twine. Put the "ends" into your friend's hand and close his or her palm over them. Pull the real ends away from each other with a quick motion and the teased strands will come together to make one piece of twine!

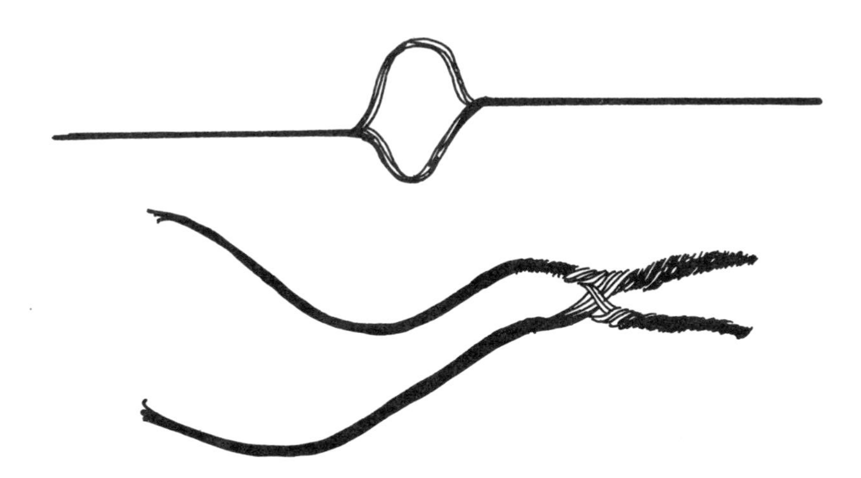

## * ESMERELDA'S MAGICAL STRING

*What You'll Need*

Table salt
Piece of string about 6 to 8 inches long
Ice cube

"My friend Esmerelda is a witch," you announce matter-of-factly as you show your friends an ordinary ice cube on a plate. "She gave me a magic string as a token of her good faith. This string has special powers. I can use it to pick up anything I want. I'll start by picking up this ice cube." You take an ordinary piece of string—let someone examine it to prove the point—and lay it across the top of the ice cube. "Abracadabra, ice cube come to me," you mutter, waving your hands over the plate. After a few moments, carefully pick up each end of the string. The ice cube will be lifted by the string!

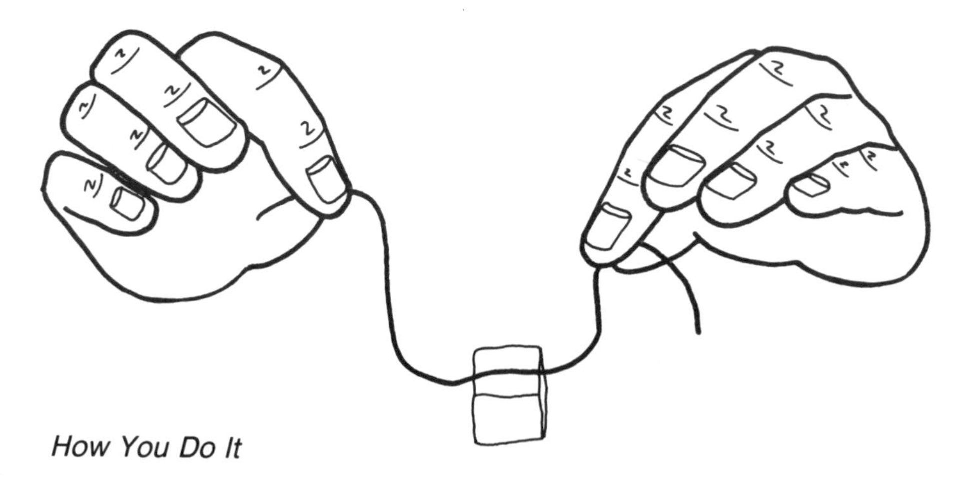

*How You Do It*

This trick requires some advance preparation. You have to sprinkle a little table salt on the top of the ice cube right before you do this trick. This melts a little of the ice. When you lay the string on top of the ice cube, it will refreeze in a few moments, and the string will stick to the ice. The bond will be strong enough so that the string will "pick up" the ice cube!

## * ESMERELDA'S MAGICAL COMB

*What You'll Need*

One ordinary plastic comb
Tissue paper
Length of black elastic
Large safety pin

"Esmerelda also gave me a magical comb," you continue, displaying a small plastic comb to your friends. "It looks ordinary, but it's not. It plays tunes from the spirit world." You wrap the comb in tissue paper and play it like a kazoo. "But the strange thing is that every once in a while Esmerelda wants the comb back. So she makes it disappear!" With that, you rip up the tissue paper and show that the comb has indeed vanished!

*How You Do It*

Before you go out in front of your audience, attach one end of the elastic to the comb and pin the other end to the inside center seam in the back of your jacket. The comb should hang down to the bottom edge of your jacket, just out of sight. As you bring the comb out, wrap it in the tissue paper. This hides the elastic and lets you hum through it to play a tune.

The next part is easy. Simply move both of your hands forward and let the comb slip out of the tissue paper. It will snap back under your jacket and be hidden once again. Then rip up the paper to show it's gone. You'll want to practice this one so that the motion of your hands is smooth. Your audience will be looking at the comb and paper, and they'll never see the elastic.

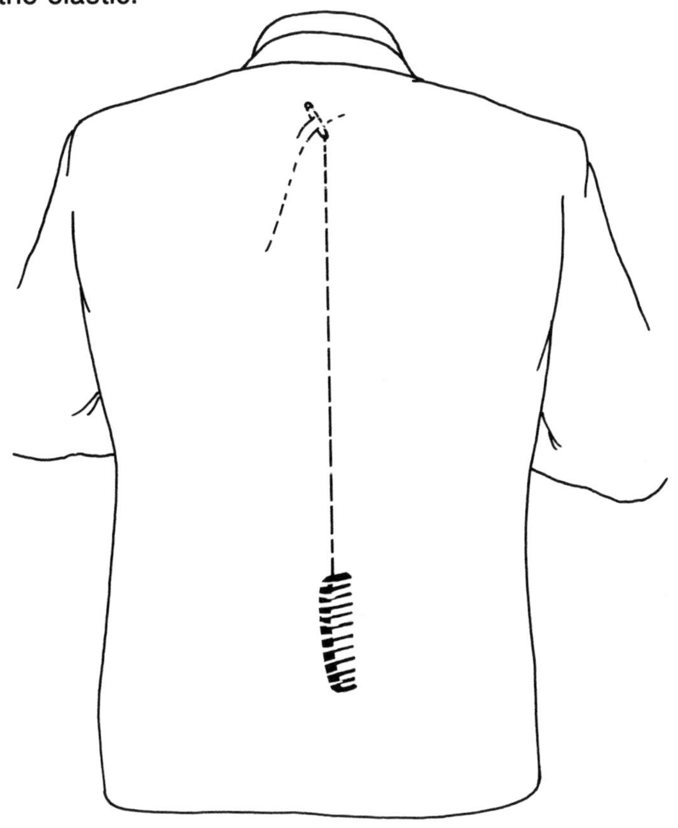

## * THE WEREWOLF'S PAPER

*What You'll Need*

A strip of newspaper, about the width of a classified column and about 15 inches long
Rubber cement
Talcum powder
Scissors

"Werewolves can be hurt by only two things," you tell your audience, holding up an ordinary-looking strip of newspaper. "Silver objects—and wolfbane. Of course, you can use garlic if you don't have any wolfbane. Now, everyone knows that if you're bitten by a werewolf, you will become one. Well, I'm going to show you what happens to an ordinary piece of paper that has been read by a werewolf." You fold the paper in half and cut across both halves about one-half inch from the middle. Make some hypnotic gestures and say in a loud voice, "Heal! Heal!" Holding one end of the paper, you let the paper fall open. It's all in one piece!

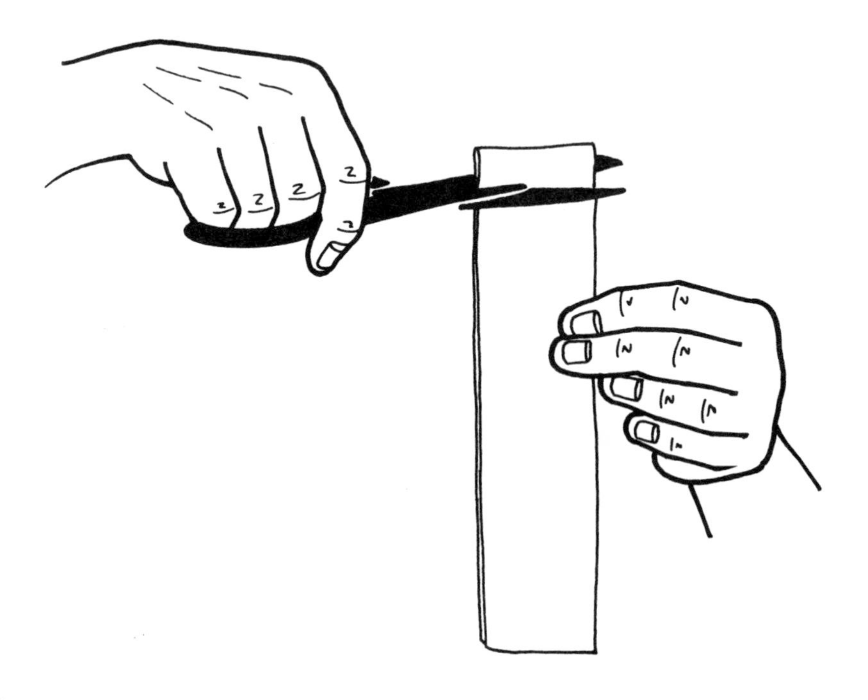

*How You Do It*

Although this needs some preparation, it's a very simple illusion. Lay the strip of newspaper out flat on a table and cover the middle of one side with a thin coat of rubber cement, leaving the ends clear. Let it dry. (It might be a good idea to prepare more than one column at a time.) When the cement is dry, shake a thin layer of talcum powder over the rubber cement. Shake off the excess. Now you're ready to do the trick, which really works by itself.

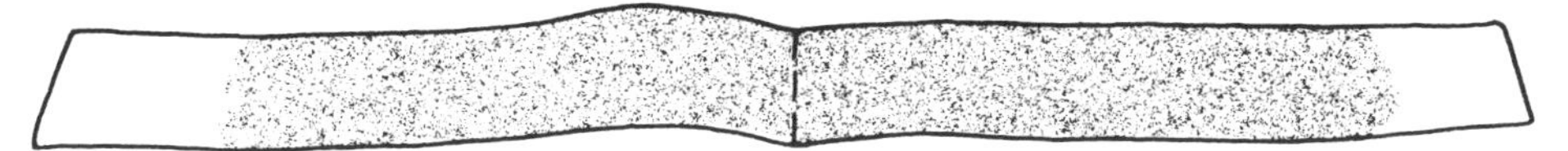

Fold the column of paper in half, with end touching end. The glue should be on the *inside*. All you have to do is cut the paper now. The rubber cement will cling to itself when pressed together by the blades of the scissors. You can do this two or three times; each time, the paper will stick to itself and unfold so that it appears to be a single uncut piece of paper. Then you can bring out the "wolfbane" and cut the paper at a point below the rubber cement coating. The paper will not stick together, proving that wolfbane counteracts the powers of a werewolf!

## * THE MUMMY'S ASHES

*What You'll Need*

Ashes (cigarette ashes are fine)

"Have you ever heard the story about the Mummy's Ashes?" you ask your audience. "No? I thought not. I'll tell it to you now. Kharis was a mummy who was brought back to life after three thousand years. They finally killed him again—this time for good—by throwing him into a fire. I happen to have some of his ashes with me." Ask a boy from the audience to hold both hands out in front of him, palms down. Have the boy choose which hand he wants to use for the trick. Then say, "Kharis's ashes seem to have a life of their own. Let me show you what I mean." Place some ashes on the back of one of your friend's hands and slowly blow them away. Rub in the residue. Chant the magical-mummy words: "Tanna leaves, tanna leaves, come back to me!" Then say to your friend, "Turn your hand over and look at your palm!" The ashes have reappeared there!

*How You Do It*

Put some of the ashes on the tip of the middle finger of your right hand. When the boy holds out his hands, palm down, you readjust their position, either higher or lower. At that point you touch his left palm with the tip of your right middle finger, getting some ashes on it. Then the boy chooses a hand. If it's the left hand (the one with the ashes in the palm), you say, "Fine." If it's the right hand, say, "Okay. Hold that one to your side and we'll use your left hand for this trick." This method of picking the hand you want while letting the person think he's doing the choosing is called "the magician's force." This way, your friend thinks he has a free choice.

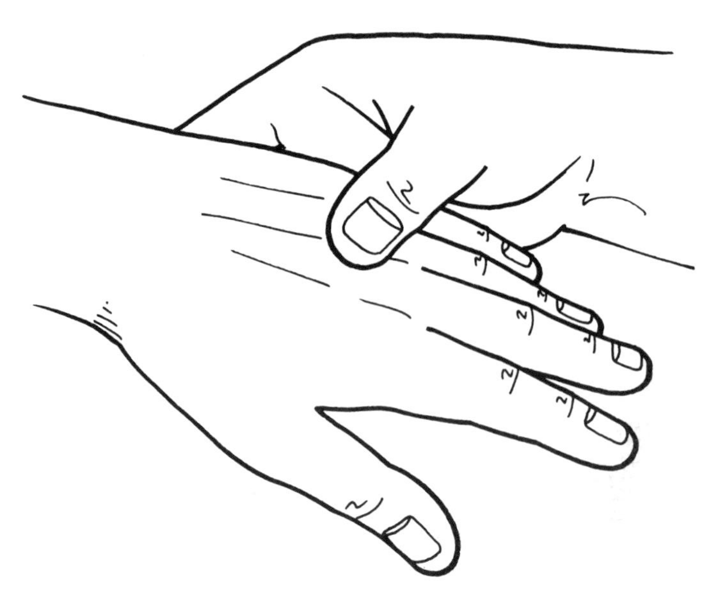

## * DRACULA'S EYE

*What You'll Need*

One wooden bead, about 1 inch in diameter
Two shoelaces (any color)

Show your audience a wooden bead with two shoelaces running through the hole in the middle. Tell your friends that this is Dracula's eye and that you've captured it and tied it up with these special strings. Then say, "As long as the eye is on the string, Dracula is powerless. But if the eye should get loose, the person holding it can be in a lot of trouble!'' Now have a girl from the audience hold her hand out, palm up, fingers open wide. Place the bead in the center of her palm with the laces hanging off either side of her hand. Have her close her hand into a fist.

Now take one shoelace from either side and tie them into a simple knot across the girl's fingers. Pull on the shoelaces and they will come free, leaving the ''eye'' in her palm! Shake your head and say, ''If you're left holding the eye, you may have some trouble with vampires. The only way to be sure Dracula can't get you is to sleep with a piece of garlic under your pillow for the next month!''

*How You Do It*

This illusion requires some work ahead of time. Instead of running the shoelaces directly through the hole in the bead, you prepare them as follows: fold each lace in half. Place the folded ends next to each other. Take one loop and place it through the loop of the other shoelace and then fold the first loop back on itself. Now the two laces are loosely linked together. Push the shoelaces through the hole in the bead. When your friend holds the bead in her hand, it doesn't matter which shoelace ends you tie into a knot. The result will be the same. The bead will come free and the laces will be straightened out and untangled from each other.

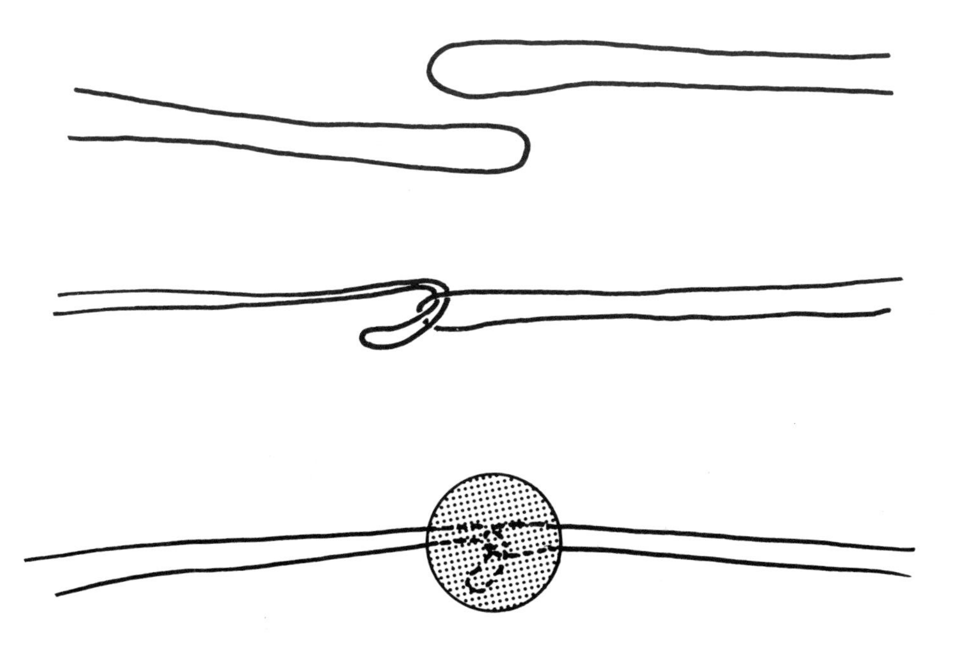

## THE DISAPPEARING GLASS

### *What You'll Need*

One ordinary drinking glass
One page of a newspaper

"This glass was once owned by a man named Zachary Rhubarb," you tell your audience, holding up the drinking glass. "Zachary was unjustly hanged for a murder he did not commit, and his ghost would not rest until it had helped the police find the real murderer. His ghost walked through walls, went through floors, and generally frightened people. This is the glass in which Zachary used to keep his false teeth. Let me show you now how it has retained some of its ghostly properties." Now wrap the glass in the newspaper and hold it up. "You can see the shape of the glass through the paper. You can even feel it, so you know it's really there. At any moment now, it will happen, though. Here it comes . . . " And with that, you smash your hand down on the paper. It flattens—the glass is gone! You reach under the table and take out the glass which has made its ghostly way through a solid tabletop!

### *How You Do It*

This trick is simple. Roll the paper around the glass, making a paper shell, but do not seal the paper around the open end of the glass. After you wrap the glass, show it to your audience. Then hold it near the edge of the table and turn it upside down. The glass will slide out into your lap (you have to be sitting down to do this right!), but you will keep the paper in your hands as if the glass were still inside. Put the paper shell on the table while you continue to talk to the audience.
When you finally smash it, of course, there will be nothing there but paper. Then reach down with your other hand and bring the "ghostly glass" out from under the table!

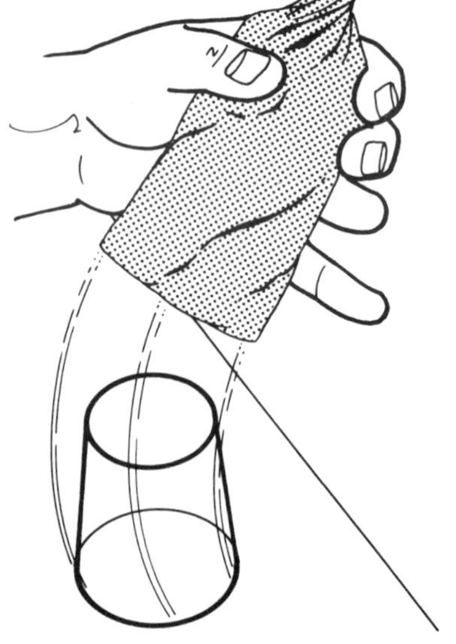

## * THE SPIRIT WANTS HER SPOON

*What You'll Need*

One teaspoon
One needle
White thread (about 60 inches long)
One white tablecloth

Begin this trick by placing the spoon on the table and telling your audience that it once belonged to a mean old woman who was a terrible miser. She wanted to take everything with her when she died, and she tried. Her television set and all thirteen of her cats were buried with her. The only thing left is this spoon, which you found under the couch in the old woman's house. Tell your audience that you're going to summon up her ghost. Turn down the lights, and the spoon will slowly start to move across the tabletop—proof that the spirit wants her spoon back!

*How You Do It*

Cover the table with the white tablecloth and thread the needle with the 60-inch length of white thread. Push the needle up through the tablecloth at a point near where you'll be sitting. Tie a spoon to the end of the thread that is on top of the cloth. Let the other end of the thread hang down underneath the tablecloth near your chair. Since the thread is so long, put the spoon on the floor by your chair. When you're ready to perform the trick, pick up the spoon and place it across the table from where you're sitting. Slowly pull on your end of the thread and the spoon will wander across the tabletop until it reaches the spot where the thread goes through the cloth. Give an extra tug to break the connection. Then hand the spoon around for examination.

# CARD TRICKS

You can learn many, many good card tricks and use them to amaze your friends. Since this book is devoted to haunting a house, we're not going to teach you all of the card tricks we know. But a good haunter should at least know how to manipulate a deck of cards. After all, you never know when you'll have to play with a full deck! So first we'll teach you how to keep a certain card on top of the deck, and then we'll show you a trick that you can do once you've mastered the illusion.

Ask a girl from the audience to select a card from the middle of the deck. Then make sure she puts it on top of the deck. Now cut the deck in half and shuffle the two stacks together, but keep your eye on that top card and make sure it stays on top by making sure it is the last shuffled card.

There are many ways to manipulate a card and keep it where you want it in the deck. This one is easy to learn and requires a minimum of practice, so for our purposes, it's ideal. Now you can spend your time on the fun stuff—scaring your friends!

## THE SPOOKY RISING CARD

*What You'll Need*

One handkerchief
One deck of playing cards

"This deck of cards was once owned by Harry Houdini," you tell your friends, holding up a deck of ordinary playing cards. "Houdini handled

them so much that they actually retained some of his magical ability." Ask someone from the audience to pick a card. That card will then levitate right out of the deck! Tell your friends, "I don't know for sure why this happens—I only know that it does."

*How You Do It*

Ask your friend to select a card and then put it back in the deck. You must make sure that card stays on top. Now pick up the deck in your left hand with the bottom of the deck facing the audience. Remember that the selected card is now closest to you. Cover the deck and your hand with the handkerchief, after showing the handkerchief around to convince the audience there's nothing tricky about it. Under the hanky, slide the selected card to the left, so it sticks out from the rest of the deck. Extend the index finger of your right hand and press it on top of the selected card. The rest of your hand is in a fist beneath the hanky. Extend your right pinky and place it under the selected card so that it supports the bottom of the card. *Slowly raise your right hand.* It will look as if the handkerchief and card are mysteriously levitating! Put the rest of the deck on the table with your left hand. Reach under the hanky and pull out—the selected card!

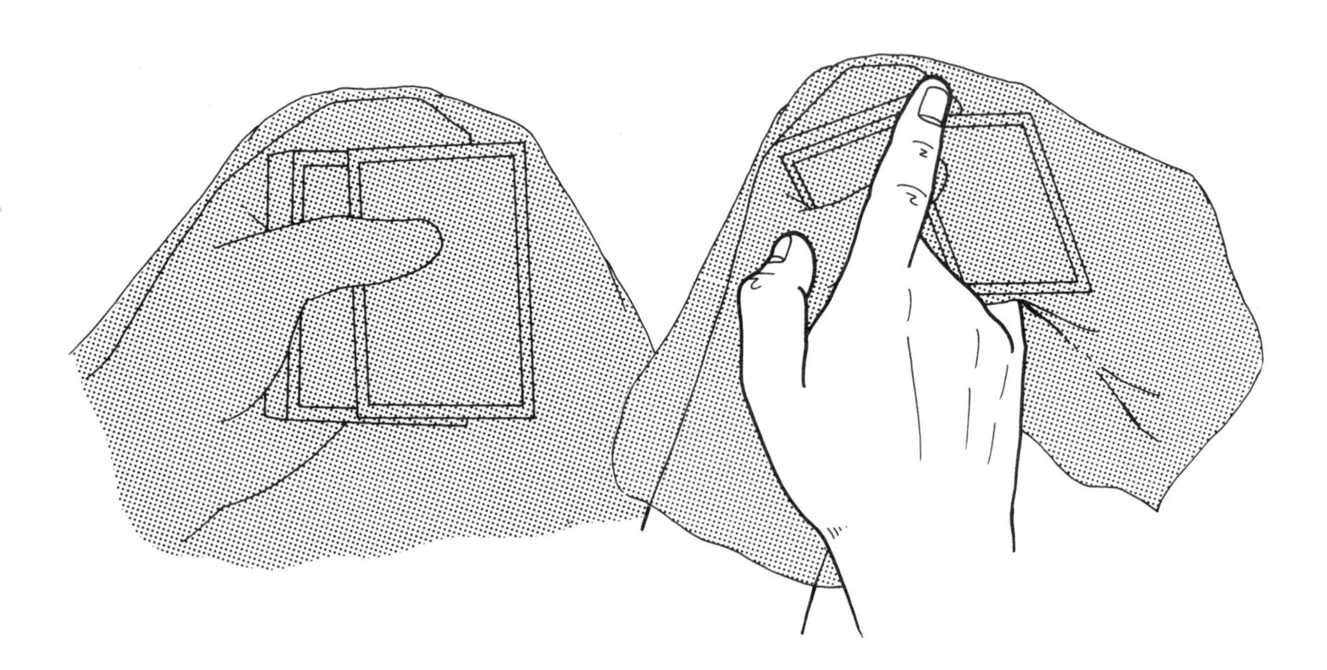

# THE MAD PROFESSOR'S LABORATORY

By combining several tricks and illusions, you can produce an effect that is far more spectacular than that of any one trick by itself. We're going to look at two of these larger-scale illusions. The first is the mad professor's laboratory. This setup will have your friends cowering in their shoes! There are four illusions that make up the laboratory, and they range from fairly simple to quite complicated. Whether you choose to use one or two or all four of these illusions, remember that the power of suggestion will do more to scare your audience than the most complicated setup in the world.

We suggest that you set aside a separate room or corner of a room for the mad professor's laboratory. And you might want to make this room the last stop on the tour of your haunted house. All of these illusions should be performed in a dimly lit room. This conjures up a scary atmosphere and also prevents your audience from taking too close a look at what's going on.

## * 1. THE SLASHING KNIFE

In the slashing-knife trick, which we explained earlier in this book, you used a rubber knife and stage blood to make it look as if you were slashing at your own wrist. In this variation, you're going to do the very same thing—to someone else! You'll need two assistants for this trick—one to be the mad slasher and one to be the victim. The victim should be lying on a table that looks like an operating table, complete with draped sheet, bloodstains, and gruesome-looking jars and bottles of bright red and

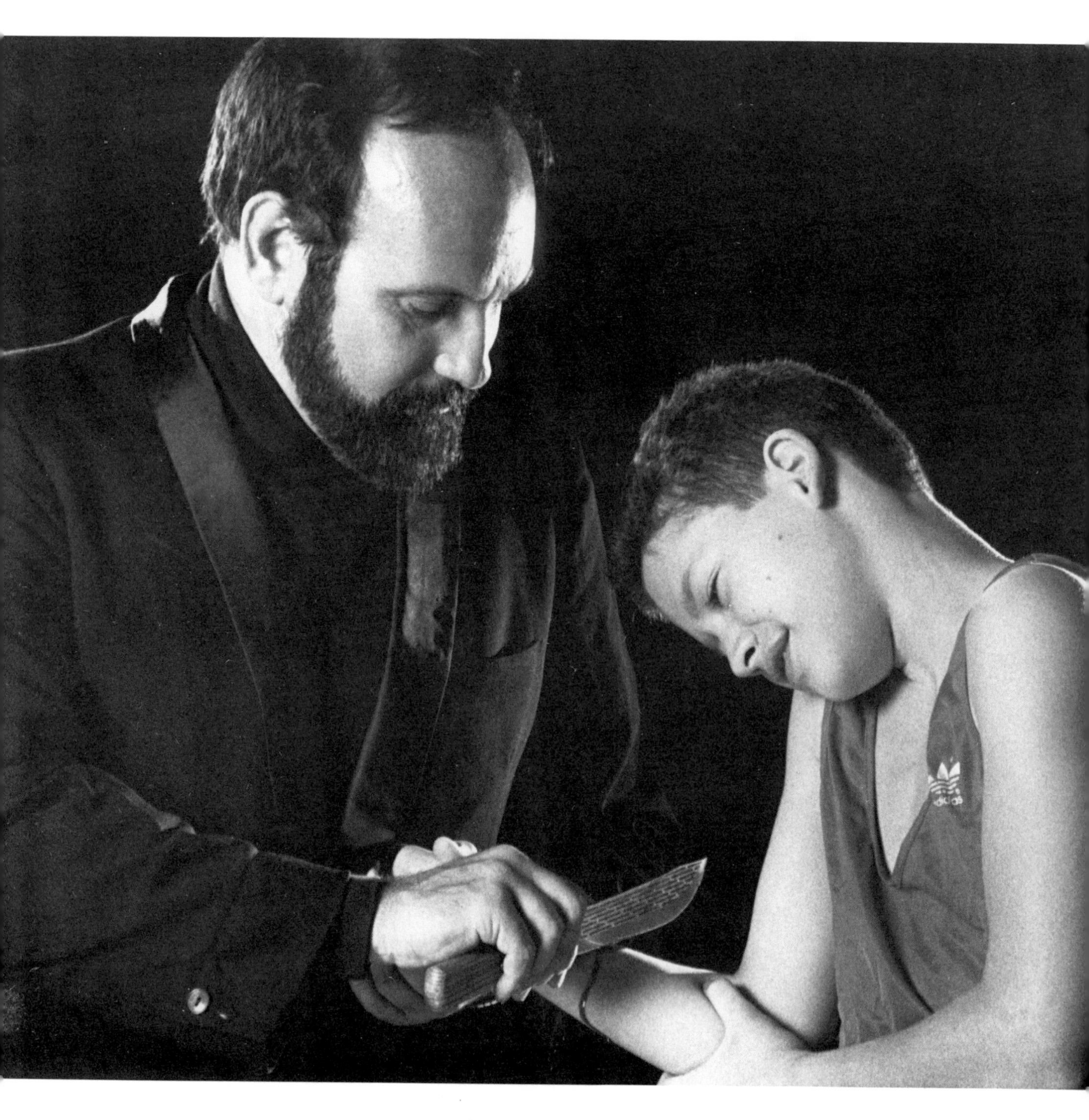

SLASHING KNIFE

pink liquids inside. (Use some vegetable coloring mixed in water to make a nasty-looking liquid.) The victim's hand should be exposed so that the audience walking by has a clear view of it.

*How You Do It*

As your friends pass by the "operating table," the mad slasher should wave the rubber knife around and then draw it across the wrist of the victim. A line of stage blood will appear and the victim should give a realistic shriek or moan.

## * 2. THE SEVERED HAND

In an earlier chapter you learned how to make the severed-hand trick look horrifyingly real. Now you can combine it with the slashing-knife trick. As the mad slasher draws the knife across the victim's wrist producing a line of bright red blood, the victim's hand will drop to the floor with a realistic thud! Of course, only you know that the hand that has fallen off is made of rubber. But we guarantee that this illusion will send your audience scurrying off to the next room in the mad professor's laboratory!!

## ** 3. THE TALKING SEVERED HEAD

Lead your friends into a very dimly lit corner of the mad professor's laboratory. "The Professor sometimes gets a little carried away in his experiments," you say as you approach an ordinary-looking table with a cardboard box standing on it. "I'm afraid this was one of his less successful attempts." Lift up the box, and there on the table is a blinking, breathing, talking human head!!

*How You Do It*

This illusion is much simpler than it looks. You will need a large cardboard box of the kind in which refrigerators are shipped. Cut the box down to about 3 feet tall. Cut a hole in the top of the box just large enough for a friend to stick her head through. Paint the box black. You'll also need a smaller cardboard box, just large enough to cover your friend's head comfortably. It should be bottomless (the box, not the head). Have your friend kneel inside the larger box, with her head pro-

THE TALKING SEVERED HEAD

truding from the hole in the top. Now cover your friend's head with the smaller, bottomless box. For even greater effect, you might use luminous paint to write a sinister message on the smaller box: "Head—This Side Up!" You remove the smaller box to reveal a "severed" human head!

You might coach your friend beforehand on what to say. For example, she might tell the audience that she was a normal girl just like them until the mad professor got hold of her.

*Note:* Make sure there is no gap between your friend's neck and the black box; otherwise, your audience will be able to see that the victim does have a neck that is still attached to a body under the box. One way to prevent this from happening is to wrap a black scarf or cloth around your friend's neck and shoulders to make absolutely sure that her head looks "severed."

## ** 4. THE HEADLESS PERSON

The last stop on your tour of the mad professor's laboratory is the most chilling—and also the most complicated. However, if you take the time to do this illusion, you'll find it's really a knockout.

*What You'll Need*

An armchair
Two pieces of cardboard, painted black
Black electrician's tape
Glue or rubber cement
Rubber tubes or hoses from the aquarium section of a pet store
Cardboard box
Two small tables
Several jars
Vegetable food coloring

The headless-person trick was first performed in the 1920s at a world's fair, and it's been scaring people ever since. Your friends will see a person sitting in an armchair. He is a perfectly ordinary person—except that he has no head. There are tubes running in and out of his neck where his head should be.

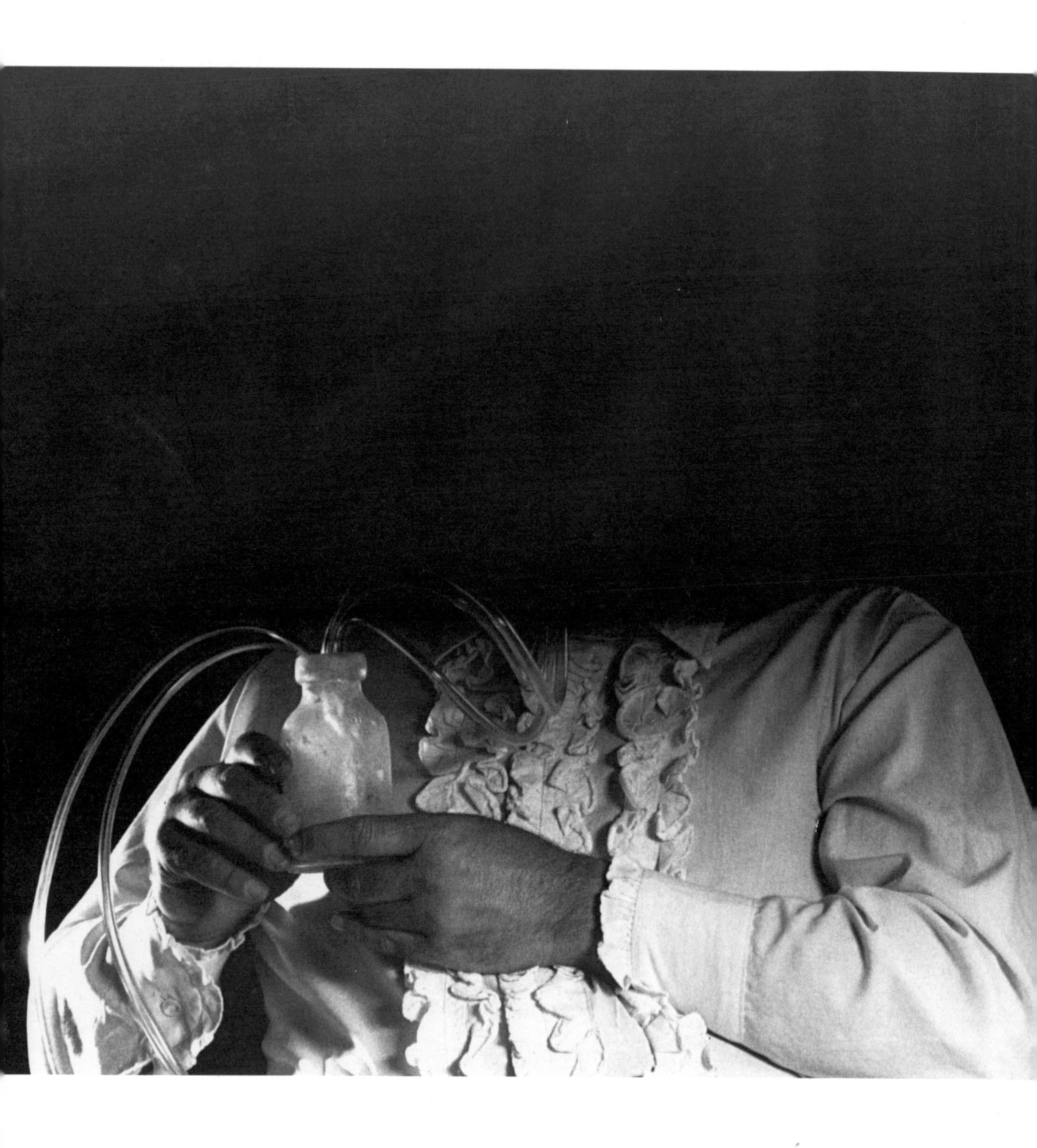

*How You Do It*

You'll need a volunteer for this trick. (You can reassure him that you're not going to cut his head off.) The man will sit in a comfortable chair. In front of his head, you will make a screen from the two pieces of cardboard that have been painted black. Tape the pieces together at a 90-degree angle, so that they hide his head from view completely. Along the outside edges of the cardboard, glue the rubber tubes. These tubes or hoses will serve a double purpose: they will hide the edges of the cardboard, and they will run into the cardboard box, which you will set on a small table next to the man. Use luminous paint to draw dials and switches on the box. The more scientific-looking it is, the better.

On the other side of the man, set up another small table with two jars on it. The jars should be filled with colored liquids—water tinted with food coloring. One fish-tank tube will run into each jar. For even better fright value, have the man hold his "head" on his lap. You can stuff a rubber mask with newspaper to make the head seem realistic. When your audience comes into the room, have the man move his hands to show that he is really alive. But don't let them get close enough to touch the cardboard, which will ruin the illusion.

For an extra zing, you can hook up a fish-tank pump (behind the scenes) to the tubes so that the liquid in the jars bubbles up. Another way to get this effect is to have one of the tubes run into the man's mouth. If he blows quietly into the tube once in a while, it will make bubbles.

Tell your friends that this is a scientific miracle and that this man will star in the next George Romero horror movie.

# HOLDING A SEANCE

A séance will make a terrific ending for your friends' trip through your haunted house. A séance can either set the stage for more shenanigans or finish off a delightfully frightful afternoon or evening. We've put together a number of tricks, illusions, and effects that work well during a séance. You can choose the ones you find most frightening and put them together to make your friends believe you really are in contact with the spirit world!

## FREEING YOUR HAND

Almost all of these tricks depend on having at least one hand free. This is the most basic and important technique in holding a successful séance. Your audience must believe, however, that both of your hands are on top of the table. So practice this technique until you've really got it down. It will be well worth your while.

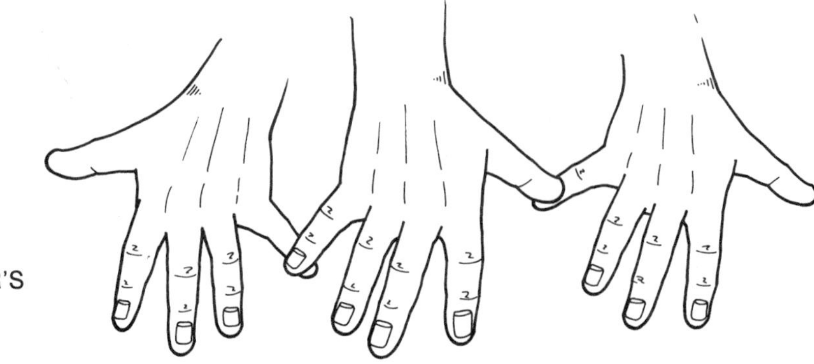

PERFORMER'S HAND

FREEING YOUR HAND

*How You Do It*

Have your guests sit in a circle with their hands on the table, palms down, fingers spread apart. Ask them to touch their pinky fingers with the pinky fingers of the person sitting on either side of them. You will do this as well. When you reach up to turn off the light—make sure you can reach it from where you're sitting—you break the circle for a moment. But that's okay, since you have to turn off the light. As you turn off the light, though, you're going to slowly move your left hand toward the right, making sure the person on your left keeps touching your pinky. Move your hand to the right until your thumb is touching the pinky finger of the person on your right. In the dark, he or she won't realize that it's your thumb and not your pinky. Now you have your right hand free to do sneaky things in the dark! If you're left-handed, you can use the same technique to free your left hand.

## THE PROP BAG

Most of the tricks you perform during your séance require props painted with luminous paint. To protect them from light until you're ready to use them, you will need a black, lightproof bag, preferably made out of cotton. Hide the bag under your chair or under the table before the séance gets going, so that you can get to it easily when the lights go out.

## SHOOTING STARS

For this simple effect, it will be best to have a helper. Tell your friends that the spirits are gathering in the room. As you say the words, the room will suddenly fill with shooting lights. The spirits are here!

*What You'll Need*

Many 8-inch-square pieces of newspaper
Luminous paint

*How You Do It*

Paint the squares of newspaper with luminous paint on both sides. Expose them to light so the luminous paint will shine in the dark. Crumple them into balls and store them in the prop bag. At your signal, the assistant will take the crumpled newspapers out of the bag and throw them around the room. The more helpers you have, the more "shooting stars" will go flying, and the more spooky your séance will be!

## THE GHOSTLY FACE

While you're in the séance room, tell your friends that you feel the presence of a certain spirit very strongly. His presence is so strong, in fact, that his face is going to materialize right before their eyes! To the astonishment of your audience, a glowing face will slowly appear right in front of you!

*What You'll Need*

One old cotton undershirt
Luminous paint

*How You Do It*

Use luminous paint to paint the ghostly outlines of a face on the undershirt. Put the shirt on and expose it to light. Then pull another shirt on over the undershirt. With your free hand, you simply pull up your shirt so that the ghostly face will appear to your friends. To make it slowly disappear, all you have to do is pull your shirt back down.

## THE GHOST DRINKS A SODA

Tell your audience that you always offer the spirits refreshments. That's how you get them to come back and visit. Put a small glass of soda in the center of the table. When you reach up to turn the lights out, free one of your hands. Everyone in the séance room will hear the soda being slurped up, but when the lights go on again, the glass will be in exactly the same place as before! "I guess this spirit was thirsty!" you chuckle.

*How You Do It*

Hide a long straw in your pocket before the séance begins. Later, in the dark, you will slip the straw from your pocket, noisily drink the soda, and put the straw back into your pocket. No one will know that you're the culprit! Make sure to place the soda within reach of your straw. For an even more dramatic effect, place two pieces of tape in an X across the top of the glass. Your audience will find it even harder to believe that the soda is gone!

## GHOSTLY ECTOPLASM

"To prove there are spirits here tonight," you tell your friends, "I'm going to conjure up some ectoplasm—you know, the stuff that spirits are made of." Say a few nonsense words, like "Abracadabra, arise, ectoplasm." Suddenly, a glowing object will wave in the air. "Look!" you shout. "It's ectoplasm!"

*What You'll Need*

One 12-inch-square piece of cheesecloth
Luminous paint

*How You Do It*

Paint both sides of the cheesecloth with luminous paint. Expose it to light and store it in your black prop bag. At the appropriate moment, pull the cloth out of the bag and wave it in the air. It will glow eerily. Crumple it up and drop it back into your prop bag before turning on the lights.

## WINTERGREEN SPIRITS

Tell your friends in the séance room that once upon a time in a tropical country, someone planted wintergreen in an animal graveyard. The spirits of the animals were processed into the candy that was made from that wintergreen. Show them some wintergreen Life-Savers and tell them that they are from that tropical country. Every time someone eats a candy, the animal's spirit is released to its resting place at last. Now ask one of your friends to eat one of the candies. To everyone's amazement, violet lights will shoot out of your friend's mouth, proving that the spirit is indeed on its way to its final resting place!

*How You Do It*

This trick works all by itself. If the Life-Savers are completely dry, they will emit violet sparks when they are chewed! It really works!

## THE BEATING HEART

Tell your audience that you had a dog for many years whom you loved dearly. When Fido died, you tried to bring him back in a séance. However, all you've been able to bring back so far is his heart. Turn out the lights. As your friends watch the tabletop, they will see a glowing heart slowly appear before them! It starts to beat, then slowly disappears.

*What You'll Need*

One plate lifter
A thin black cloth large enough to cover the bladder of the lifter
Luminous paint

*How You Do It*

Make a small envelope or bag from the thin black cloth, just big enough to hold the plastic bladder. Use luminous paint to paint a heart on the bag. It doesn't have to be anatomically correct—in fact, it's better if it's the traditional valentine shape. After the paint dries, hold the bag up to the light. Then store it in your black prop bag. As the lights go out and you tell your story about Fido, take the bag out of your prop bag, keeping it upside down so that no one can see the heart. When you're ready, turn the bag over and gently squeeze the rubber bulb a few times. Then cover it with your hand and quickly drop it back into the prop bag. Your friends will swear they've seen the heart of a ghostly dog!

## HOT AND COLD SPIRITS

Anyone who's a faithful follower of the spirit world knows that the presence of spirits in a room will make some people feel a hot sensation and others feel pockets of coldness. Explain this to your audience in the séance room, in case they're behind in their reading. Now ask them to close their eyes and put their hands on the table, palms up, and concentrate on the spirits. You or a helper—it might be better to use a helper for this trick—will now drop an ice cube into someone's outstretched hand. In the dark, the person won't be able to tell hot from cold and will probably scream and drop it, saying it was burning his or her hand. Then have your helper shoot very cold water from a water pistol. Don't soak anyone; just let each of your guests feel a drop or two of water. Even if you did nothing, their imaginations would make them feel hot and cold air on their hands.

## CRYPTIC ASHES

You can do this trick as part of a séance, but it does not require absolute darkness in order to be effective. Shuffle a deck of cards thoroughly and hand it to someone in the séance room. Ask the person to look at the top card in the deck, memorize it, and put it back into the deck. Have your friend write the name of the card on a piece of blank paper. Have an adult helper carefully burn the paper in an ashtray. Make sure there are no glowing embers. When the paper is burned and the ashes have cooled, dip your fingers into the ashtray and rub some ashes on your forearm. The name of the card will be spelled out on your arm!

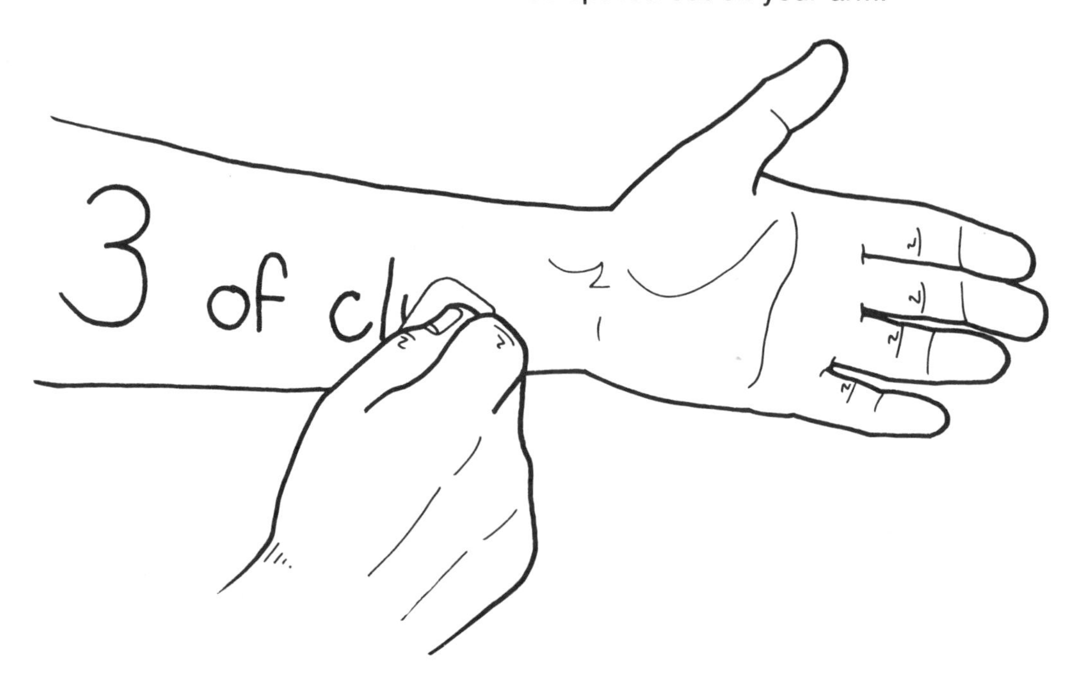

*What You'll Need*

- One bar of soap
- A deck of cards
- An ashtray

*How You Do It*

Ask an adult to use a table knife to sharpen one corner of the soap into a point. Use the sharpened soap to write the name of a card on your forearm. It doesn't matter which card you pick. When you shuffle the deck and hand it to your friend, make sure the top card is the one whose name is written on your forearm. Keep that card on top of the deck as you shuffle. After the paper has been burned, rub the ashes over the soapy writing on your arm. The ashes will cling to the soap, making the name of the card visible on your forearm!

## A SPIRIT LIGHT THAT PROVES YOU'RE HONEST

After you have done several "spirit" effects, tell your friends that you know some of them are still skeptical. But you are about to prove to them that you've been completely honest during the séance. Sit in a chair in the dark and have the most skeptical person in the room stand behind you and hold your arms to your sides. This way, you say, you can't use your hands to do anything sneaky in the dark. Now say some magic words. Everyone in the room will see a small glowing circle materialize and slowly rise about a foot off the floor before disappearing!

*How You Do It*

Before the séance, paint a small circle on the bottom of one shoe with luminous paint (see floating eyes trick, page 32). Wait until it dries. Expose it to light. While your friend holds your arms to your sides, all you have to do is slowly lift your foot up from the floor. The glowing circle will seem to appear out of nowhere (especially if you're wearing black shoes). When you're done, just put your foot quietly back on the floor. It works every time!

## THE GHOSTLY LIE DETECTOR

Tell your audience that the ghosts in the room can detect a lie from the truth. Hold up your "ghostly lie detector," which is really a small fishing weight, a rock, or a ring tied to the end of a piece of thread or string. Have a boy from the audience hold the string so that the weight hangs down. Tell him that if he lies, the weight will swing in a circle. If he tells the truth, the weight will swing in a straight line.

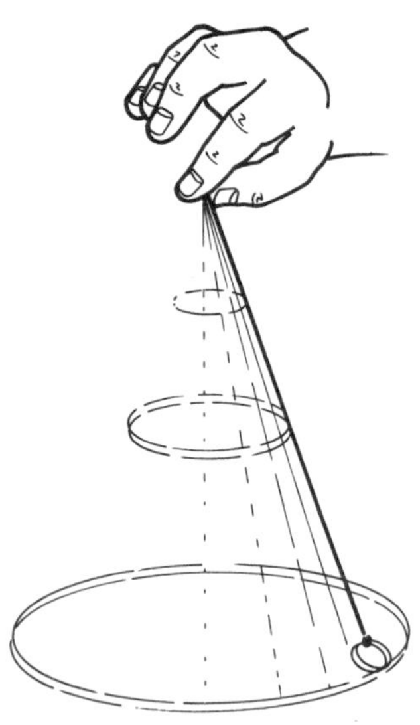

Now ask your friend questions. Ask him to tell a lie first and then tell the truth. Ask questions to which you know the answers, like his name or whether he has brothers and sisters, or whether he is afraid of ghosts. This will work with everyone, and you don't have to do a thing. The reason? There are subconscious movements of your muscles that you can't control called the ideomotor responses. The person holding the string will unconsciously make the weight swing in the correct direction. This is the same principle that makes a Ouija board work.

## THE LEVITATING TABLE

Ask three of your friends to sit around a table in the séance room. Ask them to place their hands lightly on the edge of the tabletop, palms down. "When I say the magic words, the spirits in this room will lift the table into the air!" you say. "Abracadabra, levitate." To your friends' surprise, the table will rise into the air!

THE TILTING TABLE

Ask four or five of your friends to stand around a table in the séance room. Ask them to place their hands on top of the table, palms down. "When I say the magic words," you say, "the spirits in this room will inhabit this table!" Tell your friends that under *no* circumstances should they let the spirits move the table. After a few moments, the table will start to move all by itself. The reason? The unconscious ideomotor response again. When you suggest to your friends that the table will be moving, they will actually move it themselves—while they're trying to hold it still. Sometimes a wise guy will give the table a little help in moving. That's all the better for you. But you don't need help like this; your friends will move the table without even knowing it if you give them a chance.

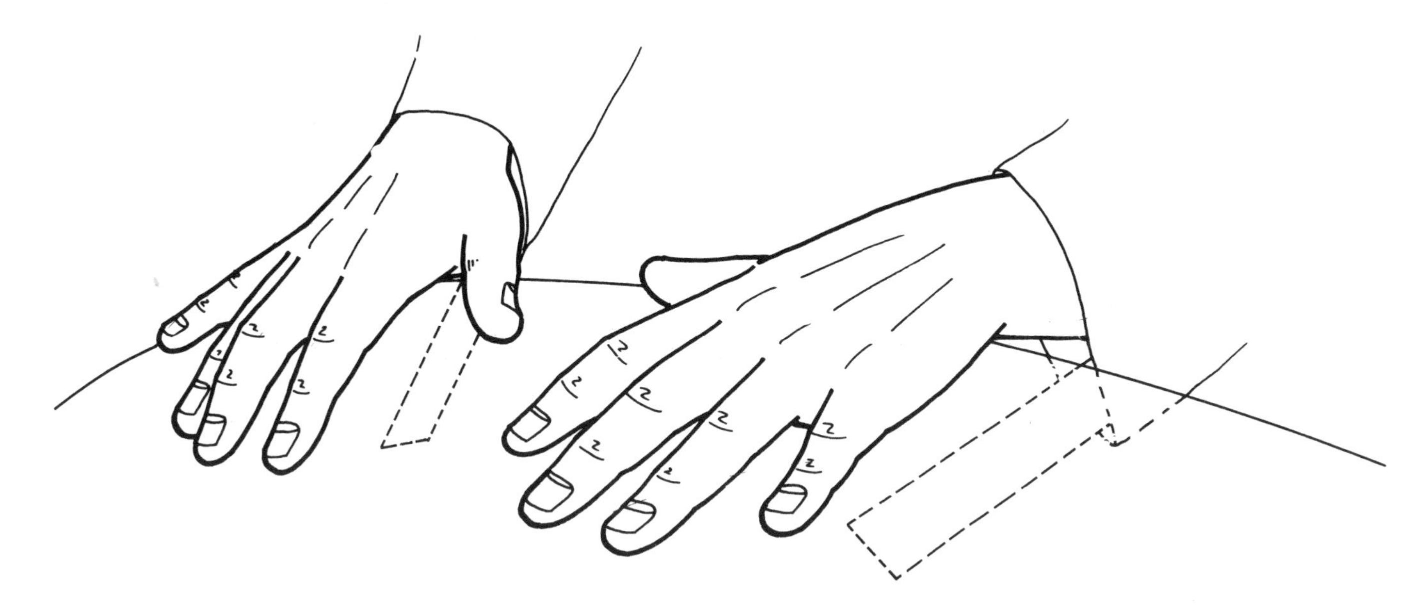

*How You Do It*

Before you perform this trick, you and your helper must strap one ruler to each of your forearms. Wear long-sleeved shirts or blouses so that the rulers will not be visible. At the appropriate moment, you and your helper will place your hands on the edge of the table so that the rulers will hook under the tabletop and lift the table up!

# IN CONCLUSION

You now have a complete working manual on how to create a haunted house at home, at school, at a church or synagogue, at camp, or anywhere you want. If you follow our suggestions on party planning, costuming, layout, special effects, illusion, and preparation, you should be able to hold a successful party for fun, or to make a little money for your favorite cause.

Remember, before you make a haunted house: think each trick through, outline the schedule for the evening, talk to your parents about it, and plan it carefully. All of the tricks in this book have been performed by us and by others many times, and all of them are quite workable. They will all fool your friends, and many of them will scare the heck out of them.

Don't expect to do every trick or effect in this book; your party would go on for hours if you did. Choose a few, plan them carefully, rehearse them, and try them out first on your family. If you don't rehearse them, they might not be as successful, and the party might not be as much fun as you want it to be.

Happy haunting!

# SUPPLIERS

Here is a list of places where you can buy magic props and other novelty items. Mention Friedhoffer when you write or call.

ABRACADABRA MAGIC SHOP
Department C-448
P.O. Box 463
Scotch Plains, New Jersey 07076
For $2.00 you will receive a catalog and a six-month subscription. Specializes in magic and fun items for the beginner. Most prices are from $1.00 to $10.00. Catalog includes over 400 products and free membership in the trick-of-the-month club.

PAUL DIAMOND'S MAIL ORDER MAGIC
P.O. Box 11570
Fort Lauderdale, Florida 33339
305-772-8067
If you mention Friedhoffer, this supplier will send you a free price list. We highly recommend this store.

THE MAGIC SHOP
Mid Island Plaza
Hicksville, New York 11801
516-822-5074
This store is a good place to buy Halloween makeup, costumes, theatrical goods, and magic tricks. Send $2.00 for a catalog.

MME
P.O. Box 1239
Cooper Station
New York, New York 10276
Send $.50 for a horror-effect price list—this is MME's specialty.

MORRIS COSTUMES
3108 Monroe Road
Charlotte, North Carolina 28205
704-332-3304
A wonderful catalog for $5.00.

HANK LEE'S MAGIC FACTORY
125 Lincoln Street
Boston, Massachusetts 02205
800-874-7400 (toll-free number)
Great magic store!

UNEXPLAINED MAGIC SHOP
235 Jefferson Street
San Francisco, California 94133
415-673-9765
Good props at this shop.

You can also look in the yellow pages under costumes and magic stores for local suppliers and shops. And don't forget to check the nearest five-and-ten for costumes and small novelty items.

# FOR FURTHER READING


Bierce, Ambrose. *Ghost and Horror Stories of Ambrose Bierce.* New York: Dover Books, 1964.

Bloch, Robert. *Such Stuff as Screams Are Made Of.* New York: Ballantine/Del Rey, 1979.

Brumberger, Tom. *Monster Maker.* New York: NAL/Signet, 1984.

Campbell, Ramsey. *New Terrors.* New York: Pocket Books, 1980.

______. *New Terrors II.* New York: Pocket Books, 1980.

Cohen, Daniel. *Ghostly Terrors.* New York: Pocket Books, 1981.

______. *The World's Most Famous Ghosts.* New York: Pocket Books, 1981.

Grant, Charles L. *Shadows #6.* New York: Berkley, 1983.

Lovecraft, H. P. *At the Mountains of Madness.* New York: Ballantine/Del Rey, 1939; reprint, 1964.

______. *The Lurking Fear and Other Tales.* New York: Ballantine/Del Rey, 1982.

*Night Cry* (magazine).

*Twilight Zone* (magazine).

Waugh, Carol-Lynn Rossel, Martin Harry Greenberg, and Isaac Asimov. *13 Horrors of Halloween.* New York: Avon Books, 1983.

Wilde, Oscar. *The Picture of Dorian Gray.* New York: Signet Books, 1891; reprint, 1962.

# INDEX

# ABOUT THE AUTHORS

Friedhoffer has studied magic for many years, ultimately receiving a "Doctor of Arcane Letters" degree from Miskatonic University in Arkham, Massachusetts. He performs all over the United States at such places as The White House, colleges and universities, trade shows, nightclubs, society functions, and on television shows. He lives in New York City.

Harriet Brown is a freelance writer in New York City. Her articles on science and the arts have appeared widely. She is also a published poet. This is her first book.